Reality Of

The Testimony of no god but Allah and Mohammed is the Messenger of Allah

Rabaa' Al Taweel

Order this book online at www.trafford.com
or email orders@trafford.com

Most Trafford titles are also available at major online book retailers.

Printed in Victoria, BC, Canada.

ISBN: 978-1-4269-3055-3

*Our mission is to efficiently provide the world's finest, most comprehensive
book publishing service, enabling every author to experience success.
To find out how to publish your book, your way, and have it available
worldwide, visit us online at www.trafford.com*

Trafford rev. 3/31/10

   www.trafford.com

North America & international
toll-free: 1 888 232 4444 (USA & Canada)
phone: 250 383 6864 ♦ fax: 812 355 4082

Acknowledgement

To his Eminence Shaikh Abdul Aziz Al Shaikh the General Mufti of the Kingdom of Saudi Arabia, Dr. Saleh Al Shaikh, the Minister of Awqaf, Call and Propagation, Kingdom of Saudi Arabia, Shaikh Muhammad Al Hmoud Al Najdi (President of the Islamic Heritage Revival Committee in Kuwait), Shaikh Othman Al Khamies (Director of Quran Centers of the Ministry of Awqaf - Kuwait), Shaikh Dawoud Al Asousi (Imam of Ahmad Bin Hanbal Mosque – Kuwait), and Shaikh Ibrahim, (Imam and Speaker of the Ministry of Awqaf – Kuwait)

Allah may preserve them

- Rabaa' Al Taweel

Kingdom of Saudi Arabia Presidency of Islamic Research and Ifta Office of the General Mufti

From - Abdul Aziz bin Abdullah bin Muhammad Al Shaikh

To the dignified sister Rabaa' Al Taweel

Assalamu alaykum, ...

I have reviewed your book "Reality of the Testimony of no god but Allah and Muhammad is the Messenger of Allah" which includes beneficial research for quotations from books, messages, lessons and sermons of known mentors and I found the book beneficial.

While I appreciate your interest in advising the Muslims and drawing their attention to this great matter, the matter of monotheism and following His Messenger (ABPBUH) I ask All-Mighty Allah to lead us to the beneficial knowledge, the good deeds and intentions and abidance by the Master of the Messengers (ABPBUH).

Wassalamu alaykum,,,,,

- The General Mufti of the Kingdom of Saudi Arabia and the President of the Senior Mentors Committee & Islamic Research and Ifta Department

3

Kingdom of Saudi Arabia
Ministry of Islamic Affairs, Awqaf,
Call and Propagation
The Minister's Office

No.: 1/7/207 A

Date: 8/10/1424 H

Praise be to Allah, Lord of all creation, prayers and peace be upon the most noble Prophet and Messenger our Prophet Muhammad, his household and companions.

I have reviewed the book "Reality of the Testimony of no god but Allah and Muhammad is the Messenger of Allah" of sister Rabaa' Al Taweel, and I found it a beneficial book compiled with appreciated effort.

Allah may recompense the author the best reward. Allah is the Omniscient and His blessings on our Prophet Muhammad, his household and companions.

Saleh bin Abdul Aziz bin Muhammad Al Shaikh

Minister of Islamic Affairs, Awqaf, Call and Propagation

5

Al Qayem, Allah-the Lord- may bestow His mercy on him says:

"The instinct of human soul knows Allah and feel it in a complete whole and in detail, then the Messengers came to remind of that and to reveal the preventing reasons from following the instinct." (2)

Thus, you educators, feed the souls of people with this great word, teach them its details, fill their hearts with its essence, which will be reflected to the voluntary organs.

This message shows the virtues of the word of monotheism, its meanings, constituents, conditions and violations. As well, declaration that Muhammad is the Messenger of Allah will enhance the impact of monotheism on the life of the individual and the society.

I pray to the Lord of the supreme throne to make my work exclusive for Him, meeting His satisfaction and beneficial to His servants.

Rabaa' Al Taweel

Friday 29//12/1424 H

(1) Noor ala Al Darb program (2) Shifa Al Aliel (2/333)

Adam

Nouh

Ibrahim

Mosa

Essa

Muhammad

Allah's blessings and peace be upon them all

The path of faith needs fixed determination

A path in which Adam was tired and for it Nouh cried

Al Khalil (Ibrahim) was thrown in fire And Ismail was prepared for slaughter

Yusuf was sold at trivial price and stayed in jail for years

Zakariyah was sawed and Yahya was slaughtered

Ayoub Suffered from distress and Daoud cried

Essa walked with beast Treated poverty ailments

Muhammad, Allah's blessings and peace be upon him

Foreword

His Eminence Shaikh Abdul Aziz Al Shaikh, Allah may preserve him, said in the introduction of this book (Reality of the Testimony of no god but Allah and Muhhammad is the Messenger of Allah):

When Allah created Adam and breathed spirit into him, he ordered His angels to bow to him. Satan who was from the jinn, not from the angels intruded among them pretending to be an angel, and when they were ordered to bow the angels did, but Satan the cursed one did not bow.

"And behold, we said to the angels: "Bow down to Adam:" and they bowed down: Not so Iblis (Satan): he refused and was haughty: He was of those who reject Faith". (34 – Al BAqarah)

The Exalted Allah says in the Al Kahf Sura "Behold! We said to the angels, *"Bow down to Adam"*: they bowed down except Iblis (Satan). He was one of the Jinns, and he broke the command of his Lord. Will ye then take him and his progeny as protectors rather than Me? And they are enemies to you! Evil would be the exchange for the wrongdoers! (50 – Al Kahf)

Satan refused to bow, arrogantly, enviously and insolently. His penalty was dismissal from the mercy of Allah and he deserved the curse of Allah. But the wicked insolence increased and his hatred to Adam and his offspring increased, and he implores Allah to grant him a respite until the resurrection day. Allah granted him a respite. Allah, the Exalted tells his story: "He said: *Because Thou hast thrown me out of the Way so I will lie in wait for them on Thy Straight Way*". (16 – Al A'raf) "*Then will I assault them from before them and behind them, from their right and their left: nor wilt Thou find, in most of them, gratitude (for Thy mercies)*".(17 – Al A'raf)

The meaning, is that Satan vowed to mislead the offspring of Adam away from the righteous path and from the salvation pathway, and to follow all means to divert them from the good deeds and to make evil attractive to them: Satan's reply was as in the verse: "*O my Lord! Because Thou last put me in the wrong, I will make (wrong) fair-seeming to them on the earth, and I will put them all in the wrong*- (39 – Al Hijr)

"*Except Thy servants among them, sincere and purified (By Thy grace)*". (40 – Al Hijr)

And Allah, the Exalted said: "*Seest Thou? This is the one whom Thou have honoured above me! If thou wilt but respite me to the Day of Judgement, I will surely bring his descendants under my sway – all but a few!*" (62 Al Isra)

Satan's misguidance and whispering continued to Adam and to his offspring until he caused the descending of Adam from the paradise and the killing of Adam's son to his brother. Satan was not satisfied. By time, he made evil attractive to them, misguided them and his guess became true. The inception of that was at the time of Nouh's people when they worshiped idols: Wod, Suwa, Yaghouth, Yaouk and Nasra. These were names of good men from the people of Nouh and when perished, the devil intimated to them to erect stones, name them after them and worship them. This is narrated by Ibn Abbas in (Sahih Al Bukhari- Imam Muhammad bin Ismail Al Bukhari The Islamic Library – Istanbul - Turkey) 6/73.

Ibin Jarir narrated that Muhammad bin Qais said, (There were good people of Adam children, and they had followers who emulated them. When they died the followers said; if we moulded them we would be attracted to worshipping and they molded them. When they died and other people came, Satan said that your ancestors were worshiping them and they worshiped them). Tabari's Explanation: Jani Albayan (Ali Jaafar Muhammad Ibin Jarir Al Tabari, verified by Mahmoud Muhammad Shakir, distributed by Dar Al Tarbia and Turath – Makka 23/639).

Thus, polytheism started with the children of Adam, because of Satan misleading them, but the Exalted Allah, with His prudence, knowledge and mercy did not leave them to Satan and his force. He sent Messengers to guide them to the righteous way and to warn them from polytheism and stray from the path, in sympathy with his servants.

"That those who died might die after a clear sign (had been given), and those who lived might live after a clear sign". (42 – Al Anfal)

"Messenger who gave good news as well as warning, that mankind after (the coming) of the Messengers, should have to no pleas against Allah: for Allah is Exalted in power, Wise". (165 – Al Anam)

"But those who reject our signs them shall punishment touch, for that they ceased not from transgressing". (49 – Al Anam)

From the *"Two Authentic Books"* Ibin Masud narrated that the Prophet said, *"No one is more fervent than Allah, therefore he barred enormity whether explicit or hidden, and no none more than Him likes praise, therefore he praised Himself"* Sahih Al Bukhari (5/194) And in Sahih Muslim, Hadith No. 2760/34

"For this purpose He revealed the book and sent the Messengers"

In the *"Two Authentic Books"*, Saad Bin Obada, may Allah be pleased with him, narrated: *"No one likes apology more than Allah, therefore He sent Messengers bringing glad tidings as well as warnings"*. Hadith No 1499.

Thus, Allah sent the Messengers to establish proof and to warn people. These missions are Allah's blessings to his creatures as they need worship more than any other need and it is necessary more than any other necessity. They are in need of the mission more than they need food, drink and medicine as lack of these, affects the bodies, but the Divine Message revives souls and it guides the individual in his life and no righteousness in the hereafter without following the message. Shaikkhul Islam Ibin Taimiya, Allah may bestow His mercy on him confirmed that in his book " *Majmoo Al Fatawa*" (19/99)

Allah sent Messengers elected from the warned people in their language to show them the righteous religion.

"We sent not a Messenger except (to teach) in the language of his (own) people, in order to make things clear to them. Now Allah leaves straying those whom he pleases and guides whom he pleases. And he is exalted in power full of wisdom". (4- Ibrahim)

Allah sent to each nation a Messenger.

"To every people was sent a Messenger when their Messenger comes before them, the matter will be judged between them with justice and they will not be wronged". (47 - Yunus)

"Verily we have sent thee in truth as a bearer of glad tidings and as a warner and there never was a person without a warner having lived among them in the past". (24 - Fatir)

They were all sent with one religion, which is Islam, and assigning monotheism to Allah glory be to Him, and avoiding any idol worship.

"For we assuredly sent amongst every people a Messenger with the command serve Allah and eschew evil. Of the people were some whom Allah guided and some on whom error become inevitable established. So travel through the earth and see what was the end of those who denied the truth". (36 – Al Nahl)

"Not a Messenger did we send before thee without this inspiration sent by us to him that there is no god but I therefore worship and serve me". (25 –Al Anbiya)

Abu Huraira narrated that Allah's Messenger said, *"The Prophets are brothers, various but their religion is one".* Sahih Al Bukhari 4/142 and Sahih Muslim, Hadith No. 2365/145.

The essence of the message that the Messenger orders his nation to obey him. Alllah, the Exalted says: *"We sent not a Messenger but to be obeyed in accordance with the will of Allah. If they had only when they were unjust to themselves come unto thee and asked Allah's forgiveness and the Messenger had asked forgiveness for them they would have found Allah indeed oft-returning most merciful".* (64 – Al Nisa)

The Messengers continued to be sent to their nations to call them for monotheism and to deny polytheism *"We sent our Messengers consecutively. Then sent we our Messengers in succession every time there came to a people their Messenger they accused him of falsehood so we made them follow each other in punishment we made them as a tale that is told so away with a people that will not believe".* (44- Al Muminun)

15

Thus, Mosa came and thereafter Essa, peace be upon them, who in their books announced the coming of the Prophet Muhammad (ABPBUH).

The Exalted Allah says: "*Those who follow the Messenger the unlettered Prophet whom they find mentioned in their own scriptures in the law and the gospel for he commands them what is just and forbids them what is evil*". (157 – Al Araf)

And He says, "*And remember Essa the son of Mary said O children of Israel I am the Messenger of Allah sent to you confirming the law which came before me and giving glad tiding of a Messenger to come after me whose name shall be Ahmad*". (6 – Al Saff)

After Essa, peace be upon him, was raised, and before the Prophet's mission, the people went astray and they fell in polytheism except few of them.

Then the Prophet Muhammad (ABPBUH) was sent, who said, "*O people, I am just an offered mercy*". (Narrated by Al Hakim – Good Hadith).

It was narrated in Sahih Muslim as "*I was not sent for cursing, but for mercy*".

Muslim narrated in his Sahih that Ayadh Al Majashie reported that the Prophet (ABPBUH) said in his sermon "my Lord ordered me to teach you what He taught me, that devils diverted my creatures from their religion, prevented them from what I made lawful and ordered them to associate partners with Allah. I send you to put you to test and I revealed to you a Book that may not be washed, you read it sleeping or awake".

Sahih Muslim, Hadith No. 2856/36

With the Prophet (ABPBUH) who was sent as mercy to the world, guide to all creatures and last of the Prophets to enlighten the souls, Allah removed His detest. "We have not sent thee but as a universal Messenger to men giving them glad tidings and warning them against sin but most men understand not".

(28 - Saba)

Sheikh Saleh Al Shaikh commented on the verse (O Muhammad I sent you to put you to test and to be tested with you) as follows:

This testing for Muhammad (ABPBUH) is in fact testing for us concerning the message of Muhammad (ABPBUH) that we must believe in it; believe in its orders and prohibitions. Testing in fact is for the people in what Allah revealed in His Book and to His Messenger (ABPBUH).

Do they believe or not? Do they believe sincerely in Allah, His angels, His books, His Messengers, the Day of Judgment and the Fate.

Do they abide by the orders and prohibitions or not? This is the essence of the message.

(A tape in concomitance of creed and the Divine Law)

"Say o men I am sent unto you all as the Messenger of Allah to whom belongeth the dominion" (158 – Al Araf)

Allah sends the Messengers and His books when the words were distorted, the Divine laws were changed and each people relied on their unjust opinions. Allah's will was to illuminate the pathway, to bring them out from darkness to light, to guide them away from stray. Allah differentiated between the righteous and the wicked people. Allah granted success to His followers and made the disobedient in distress. Allah is merciful to the believers and He is careful to guide all creatures. Allah, the Exalted says: *"Now hath come unto you a Messenger from amongst yourselves it grieves him that ye should perish ardently anxious is he over you to the believers is he most kind and merciful"* (128 – Al Tawbah)

The core of his mission: To convey the good tidings, to warn and to call to Allah with insight and wisdom.

"O Prophet truly we have sent thee as a witness a bearer of glad tidings and a warner". (45-Al Ahazab)

Muhammad (ABPBUH) is the last Prophet and The Holy Quran is the prevailing Book to all heavenly books.

"Muhammad is not the father of any of your men, but he is the Messenger of Allah and the seal of he Prophets and Allah has full knowledge of all things". (40 – Al Ahzab)

And Allah, the Glorious says: *"To thee we sent the scripture in truth confirming the scripture that came before it and guarding it in safety so judge between them by what Allah hath reveled"*. (48 – Al Maidah)

Allah laid the chest of His Messenger open, alleviated his burden, imposed disgrace on who disobeys his orders, and elevated his esteem, his name is mentioned when Allah is mentioned. The two testimonies are the foundation of Islam, which is the protector of souls, belongings and honour.

(Here is the end of his word God may preserve him)

The Islamic Religion

The Creed

It consists of the pillars of faith (Iman) as stated in Iman which the Prophet (ABPPBUH) defined when Gabriel asked the Prophet (tell me about Iman) the Prophet said "to believe in Allah, His angels, books, Messengers, the judgement day and the fate, good or harm". Narrated by Al Bukhari

This is called the science of creed and the principles of religion.

The Divine Law

Basis of Iman (Faith)

- To believe in Allah
- His Angels
- His Books
- His Messengers
- The Judgement Day
- The Fate, good or harm

The Pillars of Islam

The foundation of rites, transactions, rules of ethics and all principles that organize the lives of the people and their relationships.

These are connected
- Belief
- (Heart)

No true creed without work
- Deeds
- (Organs)

No act accepted without true creed

The Creed Position

The creed constitutes the foundation of the Islamic religion, which consists of two sides; the Creed and the Divine Law from which all aspects of the religion bifurcate.

The Islamic creed is represented by the principles of Iman (Faith) as stated in the aforesaid Hadith (Prophet's tradition) "to believe in Allah, His angels, books, Messengers, the judgement day and the fate; good or harm".

The Divine Law (Islamic Sharia) is the system from which the creed principles stem, and on which they depend.

Sharia explains the worships rites, transactions, rules of ethics and the other sides that organize the life of people and their relationships, which are called the secondary or practical judgements.

The relationship between the creed and sharia in Islam is inseparable, as well as faith and the religion of Islam . The branches may not grow without roots.

Dr. Saleh Al Shaikh said; "*concomitance between the creed and sharia means that belief and act are inseparable as there is no true creed without deed and no deed may be accepted without true creed*".

"*Whoever works righteousness man or woman and has faith verily to him will we give a new life and life that is good and pure and we will bestow on such their reward according to the best of their actions*". (97 – Al Nahl)

The Prophet (ABPBUH) said; "*surely, deeds are but the intentions (behind them) and surely everyone will have a reward suitable to what he intended*".

The Heart is the master of all organs

The Heart is the dwelling of faith

SheikhMuhammad Bin Saleh Al Othaimeen, Allah may bestow His mercy upon him cited the verse "*they say: "our hearts are under veils from that to which you invite us, and in our ears is a deafness and between us and thee is a screen: so do for us we shall do*". (5 - Fussilat)

Thus, the heart is the center of comprehension

Psychologists confirm that the human being consists of 5 main parts

1. Body

It is the least important and the proof that it is vanishing

Independent dynamic unit dwelling three organs and it departs the body when the body dies

2. Soul

Similar to soul as the Prophet says, "Come out you and psych" and it may include the body and soul. Allah says; "if you enter houses salute yourselves" (Al Nur 61)

3. Self

4. Mind

It is the secretary of the heart distinguishes between the beneficial and the harmful.

The master of the organs. It contains love, hatred, loyalty and enmity. Without feeding, it with faith life will be unbearable.

5. Heart

"Such concomitance is evident in the Iman (Faith) covenant, and in the origin of religion in that the two testimonies achieve concomitance between belief and deed, between the true creed and the other rules of Islam, as well between the testimony and the second testimony the same concomitance among creed, deed and sharia" (1).

The end of his word, Allah may preserve him.

Thus, the creed is the foundation on which sharia is based and according to its integrity uprightness to the religion of Allah will be. Allah, the Exalted says: *"Those who say our Lord is Allah and further stand straight and steadfast"*. (30 - Fusssilat)

This means that who proclaim the oneness of Allah, and obey His orders will win in the earthly life and in the hereafter.

Muslim narrated that; Sufian bin Abdulla Al Thaqafi said; O the Messenger of Alllah tell me in Islam something I ask about it after you, he said; *"Say I have faith in Allah and be straight"*.

The creed is the basis

Shaikh Al Islam Ibin Taimiya, Allah may bestow His Mercy on him said; *"the origin of religion is in fact the hidden matters of sciences and deeds and the apparent deeds will not be good without them"* as the Prophet (ABPBUH) said in the Hadith which Ahmad narrated in his Musnad *"Islam is openly and faith is in the heart"*.

The Prophet (ABPBUH) said in the Hadith as narrated by Numam bin Bashier: *"Both legal and illegal things are obvious, and in between them are doubtful matters. So whoever forsakes those doubtful things lest he may commit a sin, will definitely avoid what is clearly illegal. Sins are Allah's Hima (i.e. private pasture) and whoever pastures (his sheep) near it, is likely to get in it at any moment, and there is a morsel in the body, if it is good the whole body will be good and if it is corrupted the whole body will be corrupted; it is the heart."*

(1)Tape – concomitance between creed and Sharia – Dr. Saleh Al Shaikh

The Heart will not reach certain knowledge until it has been treated from its diseases

Doubtfulness

Lust

SheikhMuhammad bin Saleh Al Othaimmeen

Allah may bestow mercy upon him says: "*The heart may be sick as well as the body*".

Reference: Tapes on Quran interpretation tape No. 18. Al Miada Sura

Saadi says in his interpretation of the verse, "*Allah makes firm the believers in the earthly life and in doomsday*" Allah makes firm the believers that their deeds which are based on faith shall be fruitful in earthly life and in judgement day. Ibn Al Qaiem Says It means ill will and the doer avoids the right although he knows it.

This is worse than who does not know, as the former will correct his deeds when he knows, but the latter is not hoped to be corrected.

When lust arises: strong will is needed to give priority to what Allah likes over the self-desire.

Origin: Give preference to lower desires.

It means confusion of just and unjust

Reason: Ignorance

Remedy: Knowledge of Islamic rules.

When doubtfulness arises: Seek guidance of certainty

Origin: Preferring opinion to Sharia

It wards off certainty

Sheikh Ibrahim Al Ansari Allah may protect him says

Temptation is expelled by patience

Sheikh Ibrahim Al Ansari – Allah may protect him, says:

Many scholars are of the opinion that the doubtful is worse and more dangerous to Islam than the lustful as the latter admits his sin and may repent but the former deems himself right and the others are wrong, how can he go back? And he strives to establish his false opinion by all means.

Introduction to creed science

Definition of creed:

* Lingually: (derived from fastening) which is strong knotting and it is used to mean covenant to make an oath binding.

What the person knots his heart on firmly is (creed). (1)

* Idiomatically: Conclusive faith and decisive judgement beyond and doubt, which must be realistic and uncertain. If it did not reach the degree of conclusive certainty, it may not be called creed. It is called creed because the person ties his heart to it (2).

The Islamic creed:

It is the absolute faith in Allah and what must be attributed to Him in His divine power, attributes, names, and belief in His Angels, Books, Messengers, the Judgement Day and the Fate with its good and harm, in addition to the belief in the good texts, principles of the religion, what the good ancestors agreed unanimously and obedience to the Prophet (ABPBUH) by following and subjection (3).

Objectives of the Islamic creed

Objective (linguistically) means something towards which effort is directed.

We mean by objectives of the Islamic creed:

Its intents and noble ends springing from persisting in it, which include among other things:

1-Sincerity of intention and worshipping the Exalted Allah alone, as One Creator.

2-Liberating the heart and mind from running in confusion that may result from

1, 2, 3 Dr. Naser Abdul Kariem Al Aqil *"Topics in the creed of Ahl Sunna & Jama'a and opinion of the cotemporary Islamic Movements"*.

Denying this creed. A human being without this creed is either:

A-Empty from any creed and worshipper

B- or immersed in deception of material only superstitions

3-Psychological and mental satisfaction, without anxiety or disorder of thinking, as this creed ties the believer with his creator and he will be satisfied with what Allah arranged for him, and his heart will be open to Islam.

4-The intent and deed will be safeguarded from deviation since the basis of faith is following the pathway of the Messengers with sound intents and deeds.

5-Seriousness in dealing with matters of life and seizing any chance for good deed seeking the reward of Allah and avoiding any sins fearing punishment of Allah on basis of believing in resurrection and in the Judgement Day.

"To all are degrees or ranks according to their deeds for thy Lord is not unmindful of anything that they do". (132 – Al Anam)

The Prophet (ABPBUH) urged us toward this end as he says, *"A strong believer is more liked by Allah than a weak believer, be careful to what is beneficial to you and turn to Allah for help, and do not wane. If you sustain adversity, do not say if I did so or so the result would be so and so, but say, Allah predetermined and He did what He wished, (if) will open the act of Satan"* (Narrated by Muslim).

6- Bringing into being a strong nation, ready to give and sacrifice for the purpose of firming its religion without any consideration for the consequences.

Allah, the Exalted says: *"Only those who are believers who have believed in Alllah and his Messenger and have never since doubted but have striven with their belongings and their persons in the cause of Allah such are the sincere ones"*. (15 – Al Hujurat).

7- Achieving happiness in the earthly life and in the hereafter through uprightness of the individual and the society.

Allah, the Exalted says: *"Whoever works righteousness manor woman and has faith verily to him will we give a new life and life that is good and pure and we will bestow on such their reward according to the best of their actions"*.

(97 – Al Nahl)

There is no god but Allah

Muhammad is the Messenger of Allah

The nation will not be strong unless with following the steps of the Prophet (ABPPBUH) in his call to Islam in which he spent

The companions were educated by him and their hearts were purified with the Divine Law and with the method of the Prophet (ABPBUH)

Ten years in Madina; thirteen years in Makkah

Subjects of the creed science

The creed as science according to the community of Sunna and Jamaa includes: Monotheism, Iman (Faith), Islam, the hidden, prophecy, fate, narration, decisive judgements and all principles of the religion followed by challenging the people of lower desires, heresies and all strayed ideologies.

Read in the books of creed:

SheikhMuhammad bin Abdul Wahab – Al Osool Al Thalatha

SheikhMuhammad bin Saleh Al Othaimeen – Al Qawl Al Mufied

Sheikh Al Islam Ibin Taimiya – Al Aqida Al Wastiya

Sheikh Abdul Rahman bn Hasan Al Shaikh – Fath Al Majeed

(verified by Shaikh Abdul Aziz bin Baz)

Explanation of Tawhied / Shaikh Saleh Al Fozan – Ianat Al Mustafied

Monotheism First

Monotheism First

Dr. Saleh bin Hamid, may Allah protect him, said in his sermon:

O Muslims: when the human beings go astray of the pathway of Allah, they will get lost in the dilemma of religiousness and they will fall into polytheism and wade into the mire of paganism.

"Turn ye back in repentance to him and fear him establish regular prayers and be not ye among those who join gods with Allah from those who split up their religion an become mere sects each party rejoicing in that which is with itself". (31 – 32 Al Rum)

"Allah forgiveth not the sin of joining other gods with him but forgiveth whom he pleaseth other sins than this one who joins other gods with Allah hath strayed far, far away from the right". (116 – Al Nisa)

Minds of human beings cannot alone find the righteous way. Misery may not be removed from hearts, and distress may not be driven away from minds unless we believe that Allah is the All-Mighty, the Eternally – Besought, the King of man – kind and to Him we return.

"Nay whoever submits his whole self to Allah and is a doer of good he will get his reward with his Lord on such shall be no fear nor shall they grieve".

(112 – Al Baqarah)

"Who can be better in religion than one who submits his whole self to Allah does good and follows the way of Ibrahim the true in faith for Allah did take Ibrahim for a friend". (125- Al Nisa)

O brothers: whoever submits himself to Allah, will be saved from divergence, darkness of ignorance and illusion of superstitions. He will be saved from the deceivers, swindlers and leaders of evilness who trade Allah's verses cheaply. The sincere monotheism immunes the man from uncontrolled agitation.

O brothers, monotheism is complete submission to Allah alone and achievement to the true saying: there is no god but Allah and Muhammad is the Messenger of Allah in meaning and action, on which the Muslim builds his entire life, prayers, rites, living and death.

Monotheism in belief, monotheism in worship and monotheism in legislation will purify hearts and minds, purify deeds and determine that laws to be received from the Exalted Allah alone.

Monotheism is the beginning and end of the religion, both its apparent and hidden parts, it is the hump summit which the verses cleared, direction of prayer was set up for it, with it souls are protected, with it the land of Islam was separated from the land of atheism, and with it people were divided into happy and wretch, guided and astray.

O brothers: Concentration of the Quran on monotheism was great and it was the first task of the Messengers.

"For we assuredly sent amongst every people a Messenger with the command serve Allah and eschew evil. Of the people were some whom Allah guided". (36- Al Nahl)

"And question thou our Messengers whom we sent before thee did we appoint any deities other than Allah most gracious to be worshipped". (45 Al Zukhruf)

The Holy Quran often mentions monotheism and calls for it, and suspends happiness in the two abodes on it. It mentions the reward of monotheists and the misery of atheists.

"Being true in faith to Allah and never assigning partners to Him. If anyone assigns partners to Allah he is as if he had fallen from heaven and been snatched up by birds or the wind had swooped like a bird on its prey and thrown him into a far distance place". (31 – Al Hajj)

"Allah forgiveth not that partners should be set up with him but he forgiveth anything else to whom he pleaseth". (48/ - al Nisa)

Abidance by the orders of Allah and avoidance of His prohibitions are the rights and complementaries of monotheism.

"O ye people adore your guardian Lord who created you and those who came before you that ye may become righteous". (21 – Al Baqarah)

"Hasten ye then at once to Allah I am from him a warner to you clear and open: And make not another an object of worship with Allah I am from him a warner to you, clear and open". (50 – 51 Al Dhariyat)

Every Prophet says to his people: "*Me sent Nouh to his people. He said o my people worship Allah you have no other God but him. I fear for you the punishment of a dreadful day*". (59- Al A'raf)

"*Not a Messenger fid we send before thee without this inspiration sent by us to him, that there is no god but I; therefore worship and serve me*". (25 – Al Anbiya)

Allah, the Glorious, addresses the believers to strengthen their belief and to be careful of any flaws therein.

"*O ye who believe, believer in Allah and his Messenger, and the scripture which he hath sent to his Messenger and the scripture which he sent to those before him, any who denieth Allah, his angels, his books, his Messengers and the day of judgement hath gone far far astray*". (136 – Al Nisa)

Among the attributes of the servants of All-Merciful

"*Those who invoke not with Allah any other God nor slay such life as Allah has made sacred except for just cause nor commit fornication and any that does this not only meets punishment*" (68 – Al Furqan). Among the attributes of the believers: "*They will worship me alone*" (55 – Al Nur)

Further, Allah addressed His Messengers to neglect polytheism and to deny the people of polytheism:

"*Behold we gave the site to Ibrahim of the sacred house (saying) associate not anything on worship with me and sanctify my house for those who compass it round or stand up or bow or prostrate themselves therein in prayer*". (26 – Al Hajj)

"And this was the legacy that Ibrahim left to his sons and so did Jacob oh my sons Allah hath chosen the faith for your then die not except in the state of submission to Allah". (132 – Al Baqarah)

"Were ye witnesses when death appeared before Jacob behold he said to his sons what will ye worship after me? They said we shall worship thy God and the God of thy fathers of Ibrahim, Ismail and Isaac the one true God to him we bow in Islam". (133 – Al Baqarah)

Allah, the Exalted says: *"But it has already been revealed to thee as it was to those before thee if thou wert to join gods with Allah truly fruitless will be thy work in life and thou wilt surely in the ranks of those who lose all spiritual good".*

(65- Al Baqarah)

Allah, the Exalted says: *"But it has already been revealed to thee as it was to those before thee if thou wert to join gods with Allah truly fruitless will be thy work in life and thou wilt surely be in the ranks of those who lose all spiritual good".* (65- Al Zumar)

"Nay, but worship Allah and be of those who give thanks". (66- Al Zumar)

"Say I am commanded to worship Allah and not to join partners with him unto him do I call and unto him is my return". (36- Al Rad)

"And let nothing keep thee back from the sings of Allah after they have been revealed to thee and invite men to thy Lord and be not of the company of those who join gods with Allah". (87 – Al Qasas)

"Follow what thou art taught by inspiration from thy Lord there is no god but he and turn aside from those who join gods with Allah". (106- Al Anam)

The Iman (Faith) of the truly faithful, Ibrahim, peace upon him, said "And preserve me and my sons from worshipping idols" (35- Ibrahim)

"O my Lord, they have indeed led astray many among mankind" (36 – Ibrahim)

This is some of the Quran address.

As for Sunna(Prophet's practice) the mission of the Prophet (ABPBUH) was from the beginning to the end focused on monotheism, since he was ordered with absolute warning *"And all abomination shun"*. (5 – Al Muddaththir)

"So call not on any other God with Allah or thou wilt be among those under the penalty". (213 – Al Shuara)

"And admonish thy nearest kinsmen". (214- Al Shuara), until announcement of the Dawa (call for) :

"Therefore expound openly what thou art commanded and turn away from those who join false gods with Allah". (94 – Al Hijr)

Then after Hijra *"Have no fear because Allah is with us"* (40- Al Tawbah)

And order of Jihad (to strive) *"Those who have been expelled from their homes in defiance of right for no cause except that they say our Lord is Allah"*. (40 – Al Hajj)

Until the opening of Makkah and smashing the idols:

"And say truth has now arrived and falsehood perished" (18 – Al Isra)

Until his death was approaching *"Celebrate the praises of thy and pray for his forgiveness" (3- Al Nasr) The Prophet said when he was about to die "Allah's curse upon the Jews and Christians who used the tombs of their Prophets as a place of worship."* (Narrated by Al Bukhari)

These periods never slackened declaration of monotheism and fighting polytheism. The Prophet (ABPBUH) did not stop declaration when he was alone, or when he was besieged in the valley, or when he was chased by the enemies. He never stopped it after conquest of Makkah. All of that is documented in his biography and in his verified Hadith, and first of all in the Holy Quran.

For this, monotheism was first and it must be so in all times and places.

The 5 pillars of Islam, its great essential constituents were enacted to announce and to materialize monotheism, and to ensure it theoretically and practically. The two testimonies are confirmation of oneness, denying polytheism and following the example of the sent Messenger Muhammad (ABPBUH).

The prayer begins with "Allah is the Greatest" which means making little any thing other than Allah, followed by verses from the Quran *"Thee do we worship and Thine aid do we seek"*.

Zakat (Giving alms) is another pillar of Islam as a token for innocence from worshipping materialism "And woe to those who join Gods with Allah" (6- Fussilat) *"Those who practice not regular charity and who even deny the hereafter"*

(7- Fussilat)

Fasting is another pillar, which indicates readiness to suppress the lusts for the sake of Allah.

Hajj (pilgrimage to Makkah) is response to accept monotheism and to defy polytheism.

Abu Ishaq Al Shatbi, Allah may bestow His mercy upon him, says about that: (we know that pronouncing the two testimonies, the prayer and the other acts of worship were enacted to be close to Allah, to single out esteem for Him and to make the heart compatible with the organs in obedience and submission).

The Prophet (ABPBUH) says: *"We became on the instinct of Islam, loyalty and the religion of our father Ibrahim, truly faithful and he was not of those who joined gods with Allah"*. (Narrated by Ahmad)

And consider the invocation of the Prophet:

"O Allah I seek your protection from polytheism with my knowledge, and I seek your forgiveness for what I ignore". (Narrated by Ahmad)

O the servants of Allah: These multiple evidences could not be without the great importance of the matter, and the fear that people may deviate, when Satan's are not stopping to observe and to seduce the children of Adam.

The Prophet (ABPBUH) says: "*Allah created his servants truly faithful and Satan's came to deviate them from their religion, they prohibited them from what Allah allowed and ordered them to join another god with Allah*". (Narrated by Ahmad)

How there will be no fear and the Prophet (ABPBUH) addressed his elite companions:

"*My most fear for you is from the minor polytheism (hypocrisy)*" (Narrated by Ahmad)

Consider the saying of the Prophet (ABPBUH) "*polytheism in any people is more veiled than the creeping of ants*". (Narrated by Ahmad)

And he said: "*some people worship idols and some tribes follow polytheism*" (Narrated by Ahmad)

Al Hafiz bin Kathier, Allah may bestow His mercy upon him comments on the verse: "*This is the guidance of Allah he giveth that guidance to whom he pleaseth of his worshippers. If they were to join other gods with him all that they did would be vain for them*" (88- Al Anam)

This is emphasis on the affair of polytheism and accentuation on its concomitant effects.

Why servants of Allah, do not we warn from polytheism and its reason? Allah says "*And most of them believe not in Allah without associating others as partners with Him*" (106- Yusuf) some scholars say that this verse indicate hidden polytheism in some parts, which is often not felt. Such people even though they believe in the oneness of

Allah, but they do not worship Him sincerely and they act only for their earthly life and Allah does not need such surrender and obedience to other than Allah, how can one achieve monotheism.

If ye were to obey them, ye would indeed be pagans (121- Al Anam)

They take their priests and their anchorites to be their Lords in derogation of Allah (31- Al Tawbah)

O brothers: The matter is serious, who gives his affection, surrender and obedience to other than Allah, how can he achieve monotheism.

"If ye were to obey them ye would indeed be pagans" (121- Al Anam)

"They take their priests and their anchorites to be their Lords in derogation of Allah" (31 – Al Tawbah)

Now consider magic, swindle, pessimism, using amulets and talisman and swearing by other than Allah, seeking help from dead people, going around tombs and hanging lamps and curtains there, slaughtering for them and rubbing them. No strength or might but from Allah. O brothers: This is another form of blemish in monotheism came over some categories of Muslims who allege culture and illumination. They do not accept the judgement of Allah; if one of Allah's restrictions was set, they panic and their hearts get filled with detest. They have fellows who support them. They claim the preservation of human rights. However, with these only, the human and nation rights were lost.

They see Islam as injustice to woman, the penalties of Allah as cruelty and retardness, apostasy judgement as threat to the freedom of creativity and thinking, the Sharia judgement as threat to the freedom of innovation and thinking, and that the sharia laws all return to the ages of darkness, fanaticism and isolation. Moreover, they squeezed them in the tunnel of the abhorred terrorism.

"But no, by the Lord they can have no (real) faith until they make thee judge in all disputes between them and find in their soul no resistance against thy decisions but accept them with the fullest conviction". (65 – Al Nisa)

"Allah is the greatest: Monotheism is difficult for those who are inflicted with humiliation and subjection."Has he made the gods all into one Lord truly this is a wonderful thing". (5 - Sad)

It is difficult for those who enjoyed corruption and sank in mire.

"When Allah the one and only is mentioned the hearts of those who believe not in the hereafter are filled with disgust and horror but when gods other than he are mentioned behold they are filled with joy". (45 – al Zumar)

They ignore monotheism, subjugated in their minds, joining gods with Allah in their thinking and became dissidents from the Islamic nation in its ideology, vision and objectives. They became attracted to the east and west cultures and even they denied the history, originality and heritage of the Islamic nation.

O brothers: The blessing of monotheism is that it picks us up from confusion and from going astray to certainty, satisfaction and guidance.

"There is no god but He. Everything that exists will perish except his own face to him belongs the command and to him will ye all be brought back"

(88 – Al Qasas)

And Allah, the Exalted says: *"I seek refuge with Allah from the accursed Satan: "Verify those who live in awe for fear of their Lord. Those who believe in the signs of their Lord. Those who join not in worship partners with their Lord. And those who dispense their charity with their hearts full of fear, because they will return to their Lord. It is these who hasten in every good work and these who are foremost in them".* (57, 58, 59, 60, 61 Al Muminun)

O Muslims: Actualization of monotheism needs constant awakeness that drives away any satanic ideas in every action so that deeds will be destined to Allah alone.

Unfortunately, most of Muslims feels agitated if their monotheism is criticized, but due to its hidden meaning, they fell in it without knowledge. The experts of Islam decide that discussing the omission in monotheism is just to warn Muslims but not to judge them.

The people of Sunna and Jamaa do not accuse any one of the Qibla people with unbelief for no guilt. They often talk about the judgement on apostasy and its reasons, pitfalls of divergence and novelties.

Who teaches the true creeds, guides to it and warn from the pitfalls of polytheism and divergence he has followed the righteous way.

Loyalty : Refining the deeds from impurities such as :

Gaining Cordiality Favored Position Hypocrisy Seeking High Position praise and compliment.

What deserves monition is the erratic style and the imbalance in the teaching methods of religion as we see many school books go into the details of judgements even the unlikely to happen, but they do not give adequate consideration for the principles that people need.

Another methodical error is that the ancestors, Allah may bestow His mercy upon them, they used logical terms and the common people may not understand the principles of religion. If they pursued the style of the Quran, the people would learn better.

Ibin Hajor Al Haithami, Allah may bestow His mercy upon him.

(Publishing the science of dialectic theology should be stopped among common people in view of their limited knowledge and people should be directed to the style of Quran as it is clear and understood intuitively). "Fear Allah, worship Allah faithfully, actualize your monotheism and do good you may achieve success".

His word, God may preserve him, ended.

Monotheism

Definition of Monotheism:

Monotheism is derived from unity i.e. to believe that there is only one Lord and attribute worship only to Him.

Linguistically: It means seclusion.

Religiously: It means allocation of worship to Allah.

Sheikh Saleh Al Fouzan in his book "Ianat Al Mustafeed" said that monotheism falls into three types:

Type one: Oneness of Lordship

It is allocation of creation, provision, disposition, life, death, and direction of people to Allah. No one creates with Allah, gives, lends life and causes death.

Who recognizes this type alone, will not be a Muslim, because the polytheists admit it. Allah says: *"If thou ask them who it is that created the heavens and the earth they will certainly say Allah"* (25- Luqman)

"Say who is that sustains you in life from the sky and from the earth or who is it that has power over hearing and sight and who is it that brings out the living from the dead and the dead from the living and who is it that rules and regulates all affairs they will soon say Allah say will ye not then show piety to Him".

(31 Yunus)

"Or who originates creation then repeats it and who gives you sustenance from heaven and earth". (64- Al Naml)

These verses indicate that the polytheists admit that Allah is the creator, provider, lender of life and life-taker however they are not Muslims, if they are not of the second type.

The second type: Oneness of Godhood

It means allocation of worship to Allah alone. No prayer, invocation, sacrifice, pilgrimage or charity except to Allah and for His sake only.

This was the moot point between the Messengers and the nations.

As for the first type there was no conflict that Allah was the Creator, life lender and life-taker, except some of them who denied Lordship like pharaoh who said "I am your Lord, Most High" Al Naziat 24, but he knows in the depth of himself that he is not a Lord and he can not create. As well, communism in our time, denies the existence of Allah, but every sane person knows that this universe cannot exist without a creator and every sane person admits the oneness of Lordship.

But the oneness of Godhood is admitted by less people, the followers of the Messengers, while all polytheists deny oneness of Godhood that is they do not allocate worship for Allah alone.

Hence, when the Prophet said to them, "*say there is no god but Allah you will win*" they said "*Has he made the gods all into one Lord truly this is a wonderful thing*" (5- Sad) "*And the leaders among them go away impatiently saying walk ye away and remain constant to your gods. For this is truly a thing designed against you*". (6- Sad) "*We never heard*

47

(the like) of this among the people of these latter says this is nothing but made-up tale". (7- Sad) *"What has the message been sent to him (of all persons) among us but they are in doubt concerning my message nay. They have not yet tasted my punishment".* (8- Sad) *"Or have they the treasures of the mercy of thy Lord the Exalted in power the Grantor of bounties without measure?"* (9- Sad) They say: we worship Allah and we worship with Him others.

The type is the same in all polytheists and they have said: *"Abandon not your gods, abandon neither wadd nor suwa neither yaghuth nor yauq nor Nasr"*

(23- Nuh)

Similarly, the worshippers of tombs today, they say: Do not abandon Al Hassan, Al Hussain and Al Badawi. Do not obey those who call for abandonment of tombs worshipping. The type is the same: *"Abandon not your gods, abandon neither wadd nor suwa neither yaghuth nor yauq not Nasr"* (23- Nuh)

In short: The second type is the oneness of Godhood and allocating worship to Allah alone. Allah sent the Messengers and revealed the Books for this second type.

Allah, the Exalted says:

"I have only created Jinn sandmen that they may serve me (56- Al Dhariyat)

For we assuredly sent amongst every people a Messenger with the command serve Allah" (36- Al Nahl)

This type of monotheism, the oneness of Godhood, was denied by the polytheists who were the majority of people in old times and today. They refuse to abandon their gods alleging that their oracles will intercede with Allah for them.

"The evil one made their deeds alluring to them and kept them back from the path though they were gifted with intelligence and skill". (38- Al Ankabut)

The third type: Oneness of Allah's Names and Attributes

This means affirming the names of Allah without distortion or alteration as Allah says: *"There is nothing whatever like unto Him and He is the one that hears and sees (all things)"* (11- Al shura)

We have to affirm the names of Allah as He says: *"The most beautiful names belong to Allah so call on him by them but shun such men as use profanity in his names for what they do they will soon be requited"* (180- Al Araf)

Moreover, the attributes of Allah; that He is Merciful, All-hearing, All-seeing, All-Knowing. Giver and Taker are just description for the deeds.

As well description of Allah's nature that He has face, hands etc. affirm to Him what He affirmed to Himself or what His Messenger affirmed to Him. Sharing these attributes with His creatures in meaning does not call for sharing the fact.

For instance: The paradise, as Allah says, contain palm trees, pomegranate and other things known in the earthly life, but these things are different from what is existing on earth although they have the same name and meaning. The fact is different which is known only by Allah who is not resembling anything

"Whatever like unto Him, and He is one that hears and sees (all things)" (11- Al Shura).

The creatures even share the same attributes. The mosquito hears and the horse hears, but they are not the same even though they share some features.

If such differences exist among the creatures, so how between the All-Mighty creator and His creatures? We admit to the Exalted Allah, what he affirmed to Himself or what His Messenger affirmed to Him without negligence or adaption.

Affirming hearing and seeing shall not mean that they are fungible "*whatever like unto Him, and He is the one that hears and sees (all things)*" (11 – Al shura)

Thus, affirming hearing, seeing and other attributes shall not call for homology. "*Invent not similitude for Allah for Allah knows and ye know not*".

(74 – Al Nahl)

 The Exalted Allah is not similar to His creatures.

These are the three types of oneness:

*Oneness of Lordship: which is mostly not denied by any of the human beings.

*Oneness of Godhood: which is denied by many creatures and may not be affirmed without following the Messengers of Allah, as Allah says:

"*Wert thou to follow the common run of those on earth, they will lead thee away from the way of Allah. They follow nothing but conjecture, they do nothing but lie*" (116 – Al Anam)

"Yet no faith will the greater part of mankind have however ardently thou dost desire it" (103 - Yusuf)

"And most of them believe not in Allah without associating other as partners with Him" (106 - Yusuf)

The followers of the Messengers, Allah's blessing and peace upon them, the believers of all nations affirmed the oneness of Godhood and the polytheists of all times and places turned away from it.

* The third type is affirmed by the people of Sunnah and Jamaa. They affirmed the attributes of Allah and it was distorted by Mutazilah, Ashaira who negated it totally or partially. The important thing is to know the opinion of the people of Sunnah and Jamaa.

Parting monotheism into these three types is taken from the Quran and Sunnah, but not innovated as some astray say today *"Their intention is to extinguish Allah's light by blowing with their mouths. But Allah will complete (the revelation of) His light even though the unbelievers may detest it"* (8 – Al Saff)

The source of this parting is not the science of dialectic theology, which is the source of the creed of those neglected ones who talk without knowledge. It is concluded from the Quran and Sunna. The verses that talk about the deeds and attributes of Allah they are on oneness of Lordship and the verses that talk about worship of Allah alone are on Godhood oneness.

His speech, Allah may protect him, ended

Oneness of Godhood is allocating three things to Allah:

(Said Shaikah Muhammad bin Saleh Al Othaimeen, Allah may bestow His mercy upon him)

Supremacy

Allah says:

"To Allah belongs the dominion of the heavens and the earth"

(27 – Al Jathiya)

Creation

Disposition

Allah says:

"Is it not His to create and govern?"

(54 – Al Araf)

Allah says:

"Is it not His to create and govern?"

(54 – Al Araf)

Reasons of establishing monotheism in the heart

Monotheism is like a plant that grows in the heart of the believer. Its growth and beauty increases if it was irrigated with obedience which draws the man closer to All-Mighty Allah, so that love to his Lord increases, his fear from Him grows and his reliance on Him will be intensified. Amongst the reasons that cultivate monotheism in the heart are the following

1-Obedience in quest of Allah's favor

2-Avoiding sins fearing the penalty of Allah

3-Contemplating the supremacy of Allah on heavens and on earth.

4-Learning the names and attributes of Allah and their indication for His glory

and perfection.

5-Gaining useful knowledge and practicing it.

6-Reading the Quran and understanding its meanings and implications.

7-Drawing close to Allah through additional acts of worship after performing the ordainments

8-Mentioning Allah constantly in all conditions

9-Giving priority to what Allah likes when several desired acts appear.

10-Contemplating the blessings of Allah and considering His favors to mankind.

11-Complete subjection to Allah.

12-Solitude with Allah in the last third of the night, reading the Quran at this time and asking Allah forgiveness and repentance.

Among reasons of establishing monotheism in the heart

Reading the Quran and understanding its meanings and implications

Sheikh Saleh bin Fouzan Al Fouzan, Allah may protect him, comments on the Sura of Baqarah: "*And this is a great Sura which contains profuse facts on creed, judgements and stories of old nations*". The Prophet (ABPBUH) urged us to read it and he said, "*learn the Sura of Baqarah. Its taking is blessing, its skipping is loss and Satan cannot bear it*" as shown in the Hadith also: "*Satan keeps away from a home in which the Sura of Baqarah is read*". Learning and taking it means: Reading it correctly and understanding its meanings to be practiced. One of the companions of the Prophet said: "*we do not read ten verses more until we understand their meanings and practice them, then we learn both knowledge and practice*".

This is what is meant by learning the Sura of Baqarah and the other Suras.

Reading properly, learning the meanings for the purpose of practice and following".

Lessons from the Quran (page 66)

13-Socializing with people of goodness and knowledge to benefit from their direction.

14-Avoiding any reason that may separate the heart from Allah.

15-Abandonment of unnecessary talk, food, companionship and looking.

16-Like for your brother what you like for yourself and toil for that.

17-Freeness of the heart from hatred, envy, insolence and arrogance towards believers.

18-Acceptance of Allah's disposition.

19-Thanking Allah for His blessings and patience on misfortunes.

20-Going back to Allah if an evil was committed.

21-Increasing good deeds such as charity, good conduct and maintenance of blood relations.

22-Following the Prophet (ABPBUH) in every major or minor deed.

23-Fighting for the cause of Allah (Jihad)

24-Halal (lawful) eating and drinking.

25-Ordering good deeds and forbidding evil deeds.

Chapter 1
The virtues of there is no god but Allah

A good word

Al Saadi, Allah may bestow His mercy upon him in interpreting *"Good word"* said: *"It is the declaration that there is no god but Allah, like a good tree its roots established in the earth, its branches in the air and giving fruit. Similarly is the plant of faith, it is rooted in the heart of the believer, its branches are the good deeds directed always to Allah and the fruit is the words and deeds that benefit the believers".*

Allah, the Exalted says: *"When thy Lord drew forth from the children of Adam from their loins, their descendants and made them testify concerning themselves saying"*, *"Am I not your Lord,"* they said: *"Yea! We do testify lest ye should say on the Day of Judgement"*: *"Of this we never mindful".* (172 – Al Araf)

"Or lest ye soul say: Our father before us may have taken false Gods, but we are their descendants after them, wilt thou then destroy us because of the deeds of men who were futile?" (173 – Al Araf)

Good ethics

(Conduct)

Good deed

(Organs)

Good words

(Tongue)

Seed

(Instinct)

Earth

(Heart)

The virtues of there is no god but Allah

There is no god but Allah (The best among the four phrases; glory be to Allah, praise be to Allah, there is no god but Allah, and Allah is the Greatest).

For the sake of this word, mankind was created, Messengers were sent and Divine Books were revealed.

Then people were parted to believers and unbelievers, happy people of the paradise and unhappy people of the hell. It is also:

- The most trustworthy handhold
- The word of protection (Taqwa) (Piety)
- The greatest pillar of religion (Islam)
- The pathway to win paradise and to escape hell.
- The word of testimony and the key to the door of happiness.
- The principle of the religion and its summit.
- Virtues from Quran and Sunna:

"Sees thou not how Allah sets forth a parable a goodly word like a goodly tree whose root is firmly fixed and its branches reach to the heavens". (24 - Ibrahim)

"Not a Messenger did we send before thee without this inspiration sent by us to him that there is no god but I therefore worship and serve me". (25 – Al Anbiya)

The word

of protection

The trustworthy

Handhold

Al Saadi said in interpretation of (they scorned

writing "*In the name of Allah the Most Gracious, the Most Merciful*") and they disdained entrance of the Prophet (ABPBUH) and the believers in that year so that people will not say they entered Makkah opening". The believers did not retaliate, but they abided by the conditions and did not consider what was said and they gave the word "there is no god but Allah" its right.

Ibin Othaimeen, Allah may bestow His mercy upon him said in interpretation of the verse "*Has grasped the trustworthy handhold*" who holds tightly the strong tie to escape the hell.

Righteous

Invocation

Al Saadi said: This means allocation of worship and invocation to Allah alone and godhood of else is false. Surviving word

"*And who turns away from the religion of Ibrahim but such a one who makes fool of himself ----*" Al Saadi said; this word is still existing in the children of Ibrahim and it is eternal.

* The greatest blessing of Allah to His servants: Sufian bin Oyayna said: The greatest blessing of Allah to His creatures is that He acquainted them with "there is no god but Allah".

* The trustworthy handhold: Who clings to it escapes and who will not hold it firmly will perish. Allah says:

"Whoever rejects evil and believes in Allah hath grasped the most trustworthy handhold that never breaks and Allah heareth and knoweth all things."

(256 – Al Fath)

* The righteous invocation: Which was granted by Allah to the Prophet's companions, as they deserved it. so He said;

"For him alone is prayer in truth any others that they call upon besides him hear them no more than if they were to stretch forth their hands for water to reach their mouths but it reaches them not for the prayer of those without faith is nothing but futile wandering in the mind". (14 – Al Rad)

* The eternal (surviving) word: It is word that Ibrahim left to his successors. Allah, the Exalted says: "Behold Ibrahim said to his father and his people I do needed clear myself of what ye worship". (26 – Al Zukhruf)

"I worship only Him who made me, and He will certainly guide me."

(27 – Al Zukhruf)

"And he left it as a word to endure among those who came after him that they may turn back to Allah". (28 – Al Zukhruf)

* *"There is no god but Allah"* nothing can prevent it from reaching the Exalted Allah.

Narrated Abu Huriarah that Allah's Messenger said *"No one says there is no god but Allah faithfully, no more than it will cause the doors of Heaven to open allowing it to pass up to the Throne (of Allah), if this person avoids major sins"*.

The Affirmative Saying:

Al Saadi says in his interpretation:

The Exalted Allah informs His believing creatures that He firms them in the earthly life when doubtful issues arise by guiding them to the righteous way and in the hereafter to be firm on Islam. In the grave when the angels ask the dead (who is your Lord? What is your religion? Who is your Prophet?) He guides them to say (Allah is my Lord, Islam is my religion and Muhammad is my Prophet).

With it, intercession is obtained

Al Saadi says in his interpretation:

Allah alone can intercede "say intercession is to Allah in all"

The monotheism word

No god but You, glory to You I was a wrongdoer

Ibn Al Qayem says: Deeds intercede to the doer with Allah, and reminds of him when he falls in misfortunes. Allah says: *"Had it not been that he glorified Allah he would certainly have remained inside the fish till the Day of Resurrection"*.

(144- Al Saffat)

Thus, Allah forgives the monotheist but He will not forgive the polytheist.

We do not say that no one of the monotheists will go to the Fire, but many of them may go to it and be punished according to their sins, then they go out of it.

It is the greatest reason to dispel distress in the earthly life and in the hereafter. Thus, when Yunus was inside the whale he invocated to Allah and his distress was dispelled. Allah the Glorious says:

"But he cried through the depths of darkness"

"There is no god but Thou, glory to Thee: I was indeed wrong" (87- Al anbiya)

It is the firm saying. Allah the Exalted says:

"Allah will establish in strength those who believe with the word that stands firm in this world and in the hereafter" (27- Ibrahim)

It is the promise for intercession:

"None shall have the power of intercession but such a one has received permission or promise from Allah most gracious" (87- Maryam)

Ibn Abbas narrated that the Prophet said:

"The covenant is the testimony that there is no god but Allah, no strength or might but from Allah and it is the head of Taqwa (Piety)".

It is the highest degree of rightness.

"The day that the spirit and the angels will stand forth in ranks, none shall speak except any who is permitted by Allah most gracious" (38- Al Naba)

Iqrima says that rightness means *"no god but Allah"*

It saves who says it from the hell.

Otban, may Allah be pleased with him, narrated that the Prophet (ABPBUH) said: *" Allah protects who says there is no god but Allah faithfully from the hell".*

It opens to its pronouncer the eight doors of the paradise.

Muslim narrated (234) that the Prophet (ABPBUH) said: *"who performs ablution and says: there is no god but Allah and Muhammad is his servant and Messenger then the eight doors of the paradise will be opened for him to enter wherefrom he likes".*

If it is weighed against the skies and the earth it would outweigh them. Abdulla bin Omar narrated that the Prophet said that Nouh told his son when he was dying *"I order you to observe that there is no god but Allah and if the seven skies and the seven earths were put in a scale and there is no god but Allah in a scale the scale of there is no god but Allah would outweigh them".*

It is also the best deed and recitation: it equals releasing a slave and protects from satans.

Abi Hurairah narrated that the Prophet (ABPBUH) said: *"Who says there is no god bt Allah, power for him, praise for him and all-powerful, hundred times daily it equals for him releasing ten slaves, and one hundred good rewards will be written for him, and one hundred sins will be removed from him and it will be a shelter for him from satan"* Bukhari 7/167 and Muslim 2691.

It is the real tie agreed upon by the people of Islam: upon it they favour and oppose. They like and hate and because of it Muslims became as one body and solidly compacted wall.

It is the highest rank of faith: Abi Huriarah narrated that the Prophet (ABPBUH) said: Iman(Faith) is some seventy or some sixty branches and the best of which is saying that there is no god but Allah. Bukhari 1/8 and Muslim 1/63.

It outweighs the scroll of sins on the Day of Judgement: Abdulla bin Umar narrated that the Prophet (ABPBUH) said: on the Day of Judgement a man from my nation will be called and 99 scrolls for him are spread then Allah the Glorious asks him: Do you deny any of these? He says no my Lord. He says: did any of my scribes aggrieve you? He says no my Lord. Then he says: do you have any excuse? Do you have any good deed? The man says with fear No. then Allah says: but you have a good deed and no unjust for you today. Then a card will be shown to him with, I declare that there is no god but Allah and Muhammad is His servant and Messenger. The man says, my Lord what can this card do with these scrolls? Allah the Glorious says you will not be aggrieved, then the scrolls will be put in a scale and the card in a scale, the card outweighed"

(Narrated by Ahmad in Musnad, Tarmthi in Iman, Ibin Maja in Zuhd and edited and approved by Al Thahabi).

The Card Hadith

Deeds are not values by their number, but by what is in the heart.

Consider the card Hadith which outweighs 99 scrolls of sins and punishment is removed.

It is known that every monotheist is having a similar card, but many are sent to hell for their sins.

What is the secret behind the heaviness of such card? Consider the following:

Are they equal?

Certainly they are not equal.

Whose heart is full of affection to Allah

Whose heart is?

attracted to others

Chapter 2
The meaning of there is no god but Allah

No truly worshipped except Allah

Sheikh Muhammad bin Jamiel Zainu, Allah may protect him said: It is denial of Godhood from others than Allah and allocating it only to Allah.

1-Allah, the Exalted, says: *"know , therefore, that there is no god but Allah"*

(Muhammad: 19). Knowing its meaning is given precedence to all principles of Islam.

1-The Prophet (ABPBUH) says: *"who said there is no god but Allah sincerely, he will enter the paradise"*. (Narrated by Ahmad). The sincere is that who understands it, works on the basis of it and calls for it because it includes monotheism for which Allah created the world.

2-The Prophet (ABPBUH) said to his uncle Abu Talib when he was dying.

"O uncle say there is no god but Allah, a word for which I can intercede for you before Allah", but he refused to say it (narrated by Al Bukhari and Muslim).

3-The Prophet stayed 13 years in Makkah calling the Arabs to say *"there is no god but Allah"* and they said: one Lord! *"we never heard of that!"* and they did not say it.

Allah says on them: *"for they, when they were told that there is not dog but Allah, would puff themselves with pride"* (35-Al Saffat)

4-The Prophet (ABPBUH) said: *"who says there is no got but Allah and denied worshipping anything else, his properties and blood will be protected"* (narrated by Muslim). The meaning of this Hadith is that pronouncing testimony calls for denying worshipping for anything other than Allah and the surprising thing is that some Muslims pronounce it, but their deeds contradict with its meaning.

5-"*There is no god but Allah*" is the basis of monotheism, and Islam is a complete system for life which is realized when all types of worshipping are directed to Allah through subjection to Him, addressing invocation to Him alone and enforcing His law.

6-Ibin Rajab said, Allah is the one to be obeyed and to be allocated for invocation and who joins a creature in these things he contradicts his saying: "*there is no god but Allah*" which indicates slavery of the creature.

7-The word "*there is no god but Allah*" will benefit its sayer if not nullified by polytheism similarly to ablution when it gets nullified by any impurity. Thus, who performs worshipping for any thing other than Allah shall be considered a polytheist.

His word ended, Allah may protect him.

The meaning of Allah

Sheikh Al Islam said: "*Allah*" is the Lord who deserves to be worshipped and obeyed, and with this capacity, He will be the mostly loved and subjected to.

He said: Allah is the worshipped beloved, to whom we subject, fear, implore, turn towards in suffering and in whom we trust. Thus, the word, there is no god but Allah, was the most truly word and its sayers are the people of Allah, and its deniers are His enemies and subject of His enemies and subject of his punishment.

Ibn Al Qayyem said: *"Allah is the One to whom hearts are directed in glorification, subjection, hope, and trust"*.

Ibin Rajab said, Allah is the One to be obeyed and to be allocated for invocation and who joins a creature with these exclusively Divine attributes, he contradicts his saying: *"there is no god but Allah"* which indicates slavery of the creature. (1)

(1)Fath Al Majied – Discussion of Monotheism

Book – by Shaikah (Abdul Rahman Hassan Al Shaikh)

Lesson on Divine Persona

Ibn Al Athier said: *"It is the attributes of Lordship"*

Abul Haitham quoted the saying of Allah: *"No son did Allah beget, nor is there any God along with him: (if there were many gods) behold, each God would have taken away what he had created, and some would have Lorded it over others! Glory to Allah from the sort of things they attribute to Him!"* (91- Al Muminun)

Allah combines all good names and His name if mentioned blesses everything

"Blessed be He in whose hands in Dominion, and He over all things has power"

(Al Mulk: 1)

Allah removes any fear and dispels any grief.

Any creature in pain who mentions Allah will be eased, any weak will be invigorated, any weak will be powerful and any poor will be rich.

Any estranged who mentions Allah will be sociable and any distressed will be relieved from distress. *"or who listens to the soul distressed when it calls on Him, and who relieves its suffering and kames you (mankind) inhibitors of the earth? Can there be another god besides Allah? Little it is that ye need!"* (62- Al Naml)

Chapter 3
The two pillars of there is no god but Allah

The two pillars of there is no god but Allah includes:

Negative Affirmative

"No god" "But Allah"

Denying worshipping Affirming worship to Allah anything other than Allah alone such as: loyalty to Allah, such as gods, equals, glorifying Him, loving and idols and false gods etc. fearing Him etc.

Sheik Saleh bin Hamaid (Allah may protect him) Said:

Worship is a major case for a human being, which he can not live without, it is a necessary matter which happens at all times all places.

This is because a human being is weak, poor and helpless.

So he is between two solutions no third of them, either to direct his worship to the All-Mighty Allah by a broken heart and a weak-self becoming a true monotheist, obeying, calm and glad or being a depressed prisoner to false worshipers to multi different gods (stone, graves, self soul, desire, money and other laws, holy men, parties, and cultures).

Yet favouring all these false gods is wrong rather than being attracted to the All-Mighty Allah obeying, guided and loving him.

Allah All-Mighty said: « Are many Lords (differing among themselves) better? or Allah the One, the Supreme? » (Yusuf 39)

The two pillars of there is no god but Allah include

The word, there is no god but Allah includes negation of Godhood from any thing other than Allah and affirmation for Allah alone certain attributes. This word negates the Godhood of many things including but not for limitation:

- Gods
- Idols
- Equals
- Masters

1- Gods :

It means anything that brings benefit or drives away harm.

"Yet do they worship besides Allah things that can neither profit them nor harm them and the misbeliever is a helper of evil against his own Lord".

(55 – Al Fruqan)

"Ibrahim said do ye then worship, besides Allah things that can neither be of any good to you nor do you harm". (66 – Al Anbiya)

"Fie upon you, and upon the things that ye worship besides Allah! Have ye no sense?" (67 – Al Anbiya)

In Sahih Al Bukhari and Muslim after Abbad bin Rabia said: *"I saw Omar kissing a stone and says" I know that you are a stone that can not bring benefit or drive away harm, had you not been kissed by the Messenger of Allah (ABPBUH) I would not kiss you"*. So nothing is sought to bring benefit or to drive away harm except Allah.

2- Idols

Ibn Al Qayem identified the false god as: Exceeding the proper bounds of subjection and obedience. It is said: He is Taghut, if worshipped, followed or obeyed beyond the position made by Allah to him.

Followed: like clergyman, magician and wrongful scholar:

Worshipped like idols Obeyed: like rulers who deviate from the obedience of Allah and if one takes them as masters allowing what Allah prohibited and preventing what Allah allowed, they are considered (Taghut) and the doer in minion.

Allah says: *"Hast thou not turned thy vision to those were given a portion of the Book? They believe in sorcery and evil".* (5 – Al Nisa)

He did not say they are *"Taghuts"*

The indication of the verse to monotheism: Is that the idols are (Taghuts) worshipped other than Allah.

3- Equals:

What diverts from the remembrance of Allah the Exalted such as properties, fame, family, wife, house or lineage etc.

Allah the Exalted says:

"Yet there are men who take (for worship) others besides Allah as equal with Allah they love them as they should love Allah but those of faith are overflowing in their love

for Allah. If only the unrighteous could see, behold they would see the punishment that to Allah belongs all power, and Allah will strongly enforce the punishment". (165 – Al Baqarah)

And the All-Mighty says: "*Say if it be that your fathers, your sons, your brothers, your mates, or your kindred the wealth that ye have gained the commerce in which ye fear a decline or the dwellings in which ye delight are dearer to you brings about His decision and Allah guides not the rebellious*". (24 – Al Tawbah)

In Sahih Al Bukhari and Muslim after Ibin Masud, Allah may be pleased with him, he said: "*I asked the Prophet (ABPBUH) which sin is the greatest to Allah? He said: To make equals with Allah Who created you*".

Thus, anything that engrosses the mind and diverts it from remembrance of Allah is considered equal and its harm is equal to the degree of such engrossment.

4- The Masters:

Those who direct against the rightness and you obey them knowing that you are not right, or failed to seek the reality while it is possible.

Allah the Exalted says: "*They take their priests and their anchorites to be their Lords in derogation of Allah*". (31 – Al Tawbah)

In Musnad of Imam Ahmad and Sunnan Al Tarmathi after Adey bin Hatim, Alllah may be pleased with him said that he came to the Prophet (ABPBUH) while he was reading the verse *"They take their priests and their anchorites to be their Lords in derogation of Allah"* and he said: O Messenger of Allah, they do not worship them, he said: *"But they prohibited for them what is allowed and legalized what is prohibited and they followed them which means worshipping them"*.

Ibin Kathier said in interpretation of this verse, *"They take their priests and their anchorites to be their Lords in derogation of Allah"* that they followed them in legalizing and in prohibition.

The word (But Allah) affirms many things including:
- Dedication of intention to the Exalted Allah
- Glorifying and loving Allah
- Fearing Allah and seeking His protection
- Piety to Allah

Allocating intention to God of creatures

Sheikh Ibin Othaimeen, Allah may bestow His mercy on him, said:

We should recall intention in all acts of worship.

For example, recall of intention for ablution includes three things:

1-Intention of worshipping

2-Intention to be assigned for Allah

3-Intention to be obedient to the order of Allah

Intention applies also to the prayer and all acts of worship.

After Abdulla bin Amro bin Al Aas, he heard the Messenger of Allah (ABPBUH) saying: *"If you hear calling for prayer, say as he says, and who asks for blessing upon me once,*

Allah will bless him ten folds then ask status for me, which is a place in paradise allocated for one servant of Allah. I hope to be that one. Who asks intimacy for me deserves my intercession" (Hadith Muslim 198).

The First Command: Dedication of intention to Allah

It means that worship shall be directed to Allah alone. Allah, the Exalted says:

"Verily it is we who have revealed the book to thee in truth so serve Allah offering him sincere devotion". (2- Al Zumar)

"It is not to Allah that sincere devotion is due. But those who take for protectors others than Allah say we only serve them in order that they may bring us nearer to Allah truly Allah will judge between them in that wherein they differ. But Allah guides not such as are false and ungrateful" (3- Al Zumar)

"Say verily I am commanded to serve Allah with sincere devotion".

(11- Al Zumar)

And Muslim narrated in his Sahih Hadith:

(who performs a deed and join others with me (Allah), I will neglect him with his polytheism).

The Second Command: Glorifying and loving Allah

Knowing the greatness and gloriousness of Allah and knowing His attributes:

Allah, the Exalted says!

"No just estimate have they made of Allah fro Allah is he who is strong and able to carry out His will" (74- Al Hajj)

"Yet they make the Jinns equals with Allah though Allah did create the jinns, and they falsely having no knowledge attribute to him sons and daughters praise and glory be to him for he is above what they attribute to him". (100- Al Anam)

"To him is due the primal origin of the heavens and the earth how can he have a son when he hath no consort he created all things and he hath full knowledge of all things" (101- Al Anam) 65

"That is Allah, your Lord there is no god but He, the creator of all things then worship ye him, and he hath power to dispose of all affairs". (102- Al Anam)

"No vision can grasp him but his grasp is over all vision, he is above all comprehension yet is acquainted with all things". (103- Al Anam)

And Allah, the Exalted says: *"But those of faith are overflowing in their love"*

(165- Al Baqarah)

In Sahih Al Bukhari, Anas bin Malik, Allah may be pleased with him said that a man asked the Prophet (ABPBUH) *"When is the Hour of judgement? He said: what did you prepare for it? He said: I did not prepare much prayers, fasting and alms, but I love Allah and His Messenger, he said: you are with whom you loved".*

The Holy Men

Sheikh Saleh bin Hamied, Allah may protect him said:

"Those who worship idols, holy men and any worshiped subjects other than Allah, they know that these will not benefit nor harm and they know in the depth of their minds that such things are unable to create, posses or dispose."

Even the holy men and the Prophets, know that without Allah the Exalted, they are nothing.

But they have uncertainty which the Quran seeks to uproot from the hearts, because monotheism is very noble.

Taking up holy men means:

1-You believe that Allah is not knowing your condition and you want from this oracle to present your condition to Allah.

2-Or you fear Allah and you want from this oracle to mitigate your fear to escape from the penalty.

3-Or you believe that Allah is not merciful and you want from this oracle to draw you closer to Allah.

Allah, the Exalted, will be angry because of that.

Allah, the Exalted, wants no mediators between Him and His creatures in invocation, fear and hope.

"When my servants ask you concerning me, I am indeed close to them"

(186- Al Baqarah)

If you are convinced that such holy men have such rank, you gave them a sort of equality with Allah.

"By Allah, we were truly in an error manifest" (97- Al Shuara)

"When we held you as equals with the Lord of the worlds" (98- Al Shuara)

The Third Command: Fear and Hope

A Muslim fears and requests Allah, the Glorious alone, as He is the only One who can benefit, harm, give, withhold, lower and lift.

"If indeed thou ask them who it is that created the heavens and the earth they would be sure to say Allah, say see ye then the things that ye invoke besides Allah, can they if Allah wills some penalty for me, remove his penalty or if he wills some grace for me can the keep back his grace say sufficient is Allah for me in him trust those who put trust" (38- Al Zumar)

"Has thou not turned thy vision to those who were told to hold back their hands from fight but establish regular prayers and spend in regular charity when at length the order for fighting was issued to them behold, a section of them feared men as or even more than they should have feared Allah they said our Lord, why has thou ordered us to fight? Wouldst thou not grant us respite to our natural term near enough say short is the enjoyment of this world the hereafter is the best for those who do right never will ye be dealt with unjustly in the very least". (77- Al Nisa)

"Will ye not fight people who violated their oaths, plotted to expel the Messenger, and took the aggressive by being the

first to assault you do ye fear them nay it is Allah whom ye should more justly fear, if ye believe". (13- Al Tawbah)

"It is the practice of those who preach the messages of Allah and fear him and fear none but Allah and enough is Allah to call men to account". (39- Al Azhab)

"Say call on those besides him whom ye fancy they have neither the power to remove your troubles from you nor to change them". (56- Al Isra)

"Those whom they call upon do desire for themselves means of access to their Lord even those who are nearest. They hope for his mercy and fear his wrath."

"For the wrath of thy Lord is something to take heed of". (57- Al Isra)

In Sunan Ibin Maja, Anas bin Malik narrated that the Prophet (ABPBUH) visited a dying man and he said: *"How do you feel?"* he said: I am hoping Allah O Messenger of Allah and I fear my evils.

The Prophet (ABPBUH) said: *"If these are combined in the heart of a man in such situation, surely Allah will give him what he asks for and dispels his fear"*.

The Fourth Command: Piety to Allah

It is achieved by quitting polytheism and disobedience, besides adhering to the orders of Allah, avoiding His forbidden things and following the Prophet (ABPBBUH) openly and covertly. Allah, the Exalted, says:

"Verily we have directed the people of he book before you, and you O Muslims to rear Allah" (131- Al Nisa)

"Allah loves those who act right" (76- Al Imran)

"O fear me, O ye that are wise" (197- Al Baqarah)

In Hadith of Al Arbadh bin Sariya, Allah may be pleased with him that the Prophet (ABPBU H) in his sermon said: *"I recommend you to fear Allah"*.

In Hadith of Muath bin Jabal when the Prophet advised him, he said: *"Fear Allah wherever you are"*

Thus, there is no god but Allah, will not be achieved until the man fears Allah openly and covertly. Therefore, the good ancestors, Allah may be pleased with them, enjoined one another with piety to Allah.

Abu Bakr, Allah may be pleased with him, used to say in his sermon: *"I recommend you to fear Allah, and praise Him with His attributes,"* reported by Ibn Abi Shiba and Al Hakim in his Mustadrak.

In conclusion of this good talk on piety and declaring that there is no god but Allah, this will not be realized except with fearing Allah, (that is doing what Allah likes) (*).

(*) The meaning of no god but Allah and its conditions – by: Saleh bin Al Oliawi

Chapter 4
The Conditions of no god but Allah

"Know, therefore, that there is no god but Allah" (Surah of Muhammad)

Brother Muslim, meditate upon this verse in *"Tafseer bin Saadi"* Allah may bestow His mercy upon him.

The faithful is who:

1-Understands it

2-Follows it

3-Calls for it before anything else

Listen to the tape of

Shaikh Saleh Al Fouzan

(The Reality of no god but Allah)

The condition of there is no god but Allah

Sheikh Obaid bin Abdulla Al Jabri, Allah may protect him said that Imam

Muhammad bin Abdul Wahab said: The conditions of monotheism are what is required from the man to know in order to be monotheist, apparently and covertly.

First condition: To know it's negative and affirmative meaning

Allah, the Exalted says: *"Know, therefore that there is no god but Allah"* (Muhammed: 19)

And: *"only he who bears witness to the Truth"* (Al Zukhruf: 86)

From Sunna: Othman, Allah may be pleased with him, said: The Prophet (ABPBBUH) said: *"He who dies and knows that there is no god but Allah will enter the paradise"*.

His saying: (knowing its negative and affirmative meaning) includes negation of worship to none other than Allah, and the second part means affirming it to the Exalted Allah without any partner.

For this Allah sent the Prophets and Messengers and upon it their call agreed.

Allah, the Exalted says:

"Not a Messenger did we send before thee without this inspiration sent by us to him: that there is no god but I; therefore worship dn serve Me". (25- Al Aniya)

And *"we sent Nouh to his people: He said: "O my people worship Allah, ye have no other God but him"* (Al Araf - 59)

And Allah said on the call of Prophets *"For we assuredly sent amongst every people a Messenger with command serve Allah and eschew evil"* (36- Al Nahl)

And Allah, the Exalted said on Al Khalil (The beloved one, Ibrahim) , the blessing and peace of Allah upon him:

"Behold! Ibrahim said to his father and his people: I do indeed clear myself of what ye worship": (26- Al Zukhruf)

"And he left if as word to endure among those who came after him that they may turn back to Allah". (28- Al Zukhruf)

Allah, the Exalted says on His decree to His Prophet Muhammad (ABPBUH) *"Your load has decreed that you worship none but Him"*.

These verses and their meanings in the Holy Book are clear indication that all Prophets called their peoples to worship none but Allah.

Consider this verse: *"Know, therefore, that there is not god but Allah, and ask forgiveness for thy fault, and for the men and women who believe for Allah knows how ye more about and how ye swell in your homes"* (Muhammed: 19)

Ibn Al Saadi, Allah may bestow His mercy upon him said;

"Knowing includes confession by heart, that is to act accordingly. Such knowing is individual duty on each Muslim". The way to know that there is no god but Allah includes several affairs:

The first: But the greatest is contemplating the attributes of Allah and His creation which indicate His perfection, greatness and glory and that calls for allocating worship to Him alone.

The second: To know that He alone created the universe and He alone is marked by Godhood.

The third: To know that He alone gives the blessings either apparent or covert and consequently He alone must be loved and worshipped.

Fourth: What we see or hear about reward to His devotees and punishment to the polytheists, calls for that Allah alone deserves worshipping exclusively.

Fifth: Knowing that the idols and equals who are worshipped jointly with Allah cannot bring benefit or drive away harm, nor give life or death, which calls for knowing that there is no god but Allah and invalidity of anything else.

Sixth: Concurrence and connivance of the Divine Books on such fact.

Seventh: The most perfect creatures of Allah; the Prophets, Messengers and devotees of Allah, admitted that to Allah.

Eighth: The established proofs of Allah, tell that monotheism is the great indication. Allah intensified His call to the creatures, that there is no god but Allah.

Thus, faith and knowledge will be established in the heart of man like lofty immovable mountains, and suspicions will not affect them, but give them power and perfection.

If you consider the great proof and the bid affair, contemplating the verses of the Quran you will find the great entrance to monotheism (Tafseer Ibin Katheer 4/147).

What the verses suggest:

First: To know the meaning of, there is no god but Allah, negatively and positively and the Sheikh stated the ways that lead to this knowledge.

Second: In his decree to the Prophet (ABPBUH) to ask for forgiveness for the believers of men and women it includes the disobedient Muslims. Imam Ahmad said: "A monotheist who dies shall not be prevented from prayer and asking forgiveness for him, for a guilt he had committed either minor or major, his affair is to Allah, the Exalted".

Third: Allah knows the deeds of the creatures and calls them to account accordingly.

His saying: *"only he who bears witness to the truth"* Ibin Katheer said: *"this is a ceased exception, that is who witness to the truth with knowledge his intercession will be accepted"* (Tafseer Ibin Katheer 4/147).

His saying (There is no god but Allah).

Sheikh Abdul Rahman bin Saadu said: *"That is he pronounced the testification, confessing with his heart, knowing what he testifies conditioned to be oneness for Allah and Prophethood for his Messengers and truthfulness of what they produced"*. (Tafseer Ibn Al Saadi 4/461)

His saying in Sahih Muslim: (Who dies knowing --------) Nawawi said in Al Iman book: who dies a monotheist, absolutely shall enter the paradise.

The Hadith, which means that who died a monotheist will enter the paradise, had many suggested interpretations.

First: What is narrated by Al Shaikhan after Obada bin Al Samil said that the Prophet (ABPBUH) said: *"who testifies that there is no god but Allah, and Muhammad is His servant and Messenger, Essa is the servant and Messenger of Alllah, His word and spirit went to Mary, paradise is truth and hell is truth Allah will accept him in paradise for his deeds"*.

Second: Muslim narrated, Jabir said that the Prophet (ABPBUH) said: *"who meets Allah, joining none with Him, he will be accepted in the paradise and who meets Him as a polytheist will enter the hell"*.

These Hadiths suggest two things:

First: A promise to go to paradise for who dies as a monotheist.

Second: who commits a grievous sin will not lose the tile of Iman, he is a believer with his faith and a transgressor with his major sin. Al Bukhari narrated that Anas, Allah may be pleased with him, said that the Prophet (ABPBUH) said: "*who prays our prayers, directs his face towards Kaba and eats our slaughtered animal is*

Muslim having the protection of Allah and His Messenger, do not degrade Allah's protection to him"

Second condition: Certainty, which means perfect

awareness of it, averting suspicion

The evidence is in the verse: "*Only those are believers who have believed in Allah and his Messenger, and have never since doubted, but have striven with their belongings and their persons in the cause of Allah such are the sincere ones*". (15- Al Hujurat)

Allah stipulated true belief in Allah and His Messenger without any suspicion, as the skeptic is hypocrite

In Sunna: Abi Huriareh narrated that the Prophet (ABPBUH) said: "*who meets Allah believing certainly that there is no god but Allah and I the Messenger of Allah, surely he will be admitted to the paradise*".

(Muslim: Al Iman book)

In the verse, "*Only those are believers who have believed in Allah and his Messenger*" only is particle of limitation and confirmation of judgement, there He said: "*such are the sincere ones*". (15- Al Hujarat)

The proof in the verse *"and have never doubted"* is indication that deed is part of Iman.

He mentioned fighting in the cause of Allah as one of the faith attributes.

Al Shaikhan narrated after Abi Hamza that he said: "a group of people from Rabbiea came to the Prophet and they said: O the Messenger of Allah, we came from a far distance and between us and you the polytheists of Mudhar, and we cannot come to you except on the sacred month. Tell us about a matter to convey to our people that it qualifies us to enter the paradise. He said: "the Prophet ordered them to follow four things and to abstain from four things. He said: "he ordered them to believe in Allah alone which means to declare that there is no god but Allah and Muhammad is the Messenger of Allah, to perform the prayers, to give Zakat (Giving alms), to fast Ramadan and to give one fifth of the booty".

(Al Bukhari- Times of Assalat Book, chapter on: perform the prayers and do not be with the atheists).

Muslim – Al Iman Book: Chapter on ordering belief in the Exalted Allah and His Messenger (the blessings of Allah and peace be upon him), the religion rules, calling for it, asking about it, memorizing and conveying it to who was not notified of it.

The proof is that the Prophet (ABPBUH) interpreted the faith according to the apparent deeds of Islam.

"I declare that there is no god but Allah and Muhammad is the Messenger of Allah" is admission that worship shall be assigned for Allah the One and Muhammad is the Messenger of Allah which is free from doubt will not prevent paradise.

Regarding this, two points should be clarified:

The first: Prevention from paradise falls into two types :

Permanent prevention

This is applicable to polytheists and negated from monotheists

Temporary prevention

This may apply to some monotheists for committing major sins on basis of the recurrent Hadith

Second: The negated prevention is not absolute, but limited

Abi Hurairah narrated that the Prophet (ABPBUH) said: *"Announce glad tiding to the people who testify that there is no god but Allah with assured faith, that they will be admitted to the paradise"*.

His saying: *"Announce good tidings"* means that the Prophet (ABPBUH) ordered Abi Huriarah to tell every Muslim he meets that he is of the paradise people.

And his saying: *"one who knows for certain"* means negating doubt and suspicion which is the subject proof of the Hadith.

What the Hadith indicates:

First: To believe in the Judgement Day with its reward and punishment.

Second: who dies a monotheist with assured faith will enter the paradise.

Third: The critical matter is acceptance of right mutual consultation, even from one person regardless of canvassing of votes.

Fourth: Averting evils takes priority over procuring benefits, and that to be referred to the Divine Law and not merely to the mind. There are many proofs, no room to mention them in this subject.

Allah commands you for yourself
And other than Allah commands you for himself
Dr. Saleh Al Aboud

The third condition: Devotion contrary to polytheism

The evidence of devotion is His saying: *"Is it not to Allah that sincere devotion is due?"* (3- Al Zumar)

And His saying: *"And they have been commanded no more than this to worship Allah offering Him sincerer devotion"* (5- Al Bayyinah)

In Sahih Al Bukari, chapter Eagerness to learn the Hadith, Abu Hurairi narrated that the Prophet (ABPBUH) said: *"The luckiest person who will have my intercession on the Day of Resurrection will be the one who said sincerely from his heart, there is no god but Allah"*.

Abu Huraira narrated that the Prophet (ABPBUH) said: *"whoever says sincerely: there is no god but Allah, no partner with him, supremacy and praise to Him, All-powerful He is, Allah will slit open the sky to see him and he will be given what he implored"*. (Amal Youm Waliala page 150)

His saying: Sincerity

Linguistically: means (purity)

In religion: It means purification of worship from the impurities of polytheism and hypocrisy.

Allah, the Exalted says: *"For Him is the pure religion"*

Ibin Katheer said it means: worship Allah alone without a partner, call people for that, tell them that worshipping is not righteous if it is not assigned to Allah alone and Allah has no partner and no equal. It means that no deed from the worshiper will be accepted unless it was purely for Him without a partner". (Tafseer Ibin Katheer4/49)

Ibin Al Saadi, Allah may bestow His mercy upon him, said: *"This is decree for sincerity and statement that since Allah, the Exalted is Perfect and He granted blessings to his creatures, He must have the pure religion, free from any impurities, which He accepted to the elite of His creatures"* Proof: 5

Allah the Exalted says: *"And they have been commanded no more than this to worship Allah offering Him secure devotion"* (5- Al Bayyinah)

Shaikh Abdul Rahman bin Saadi comments on this verse that it means devotion of worship to Allah turning away from all religions against monotheism and he mentioned specifically prayer and zakat (Giving alms), as who performs then fulfils all rules of religion. "And that is the religion right and straight" means the straight religion leading to paradise and else leading to hell (Tafseer Ibin Saadi 5/442).

The interscession of the Prophet as stated in the Hadith narrated by Abi Huriarah *"The luckiest person who will have my intercession on the Day of Resurrection will be the one who said sincerely from his heart there is no god but Allah"*. Means intercession for major sin doers of the monotheist, which was denied by some heretic groups like Mutazilah and Khawarij.

The invocation book included *"my intercession to the people of major sins of my people"* Fath Al Bary 11/443. This is clear support to the argument of the group of Sunna and Jamaa and nullity of the opinion of the dissidents.

I said: The Hadith narrated by the two Shaikhs, has a story. Bukhari reported that Atban bin Malik who is one of the companions of the Messenger of Allah (ABPBUH) and who witnesses the battle of Badr from the Helpers (Al – Ansar) said that he came to the Prophet (ABPBUH) and said: O the Messenger of Allah, I denied my sight while I pray with my group, rain fell and the valley flew between me and them, so I could not go to their mosque to lead their prayers. I would like, if you, the Messenger of Allah, come to my home so that I can take it as a mosque. The Prophet said: *"I will do by the will of Allah"*. Atban said: The Prophet and Abu Bakr came on the next day and the Prophet asked permission to enter. I gave him the permission. and he said: *"Where do you like me to pray at your home?"* I pointed to a place then we lined and he prayed two bows and ended his prayer. Then some men came to the Prophet and one of them, said: this is a hypocrite, he does not like Allah and his Messenger. The Prophet said, "Do not say that, he is saying, no god but Allah seeking the satisfaction of Allah". He said, Allah and His Messenger know best.

Concerning his saying: (Allah prevented him from fire) I said prevention falls into two types:

- Prevention from Entrance: This applies to those who die on monotheism without committing major sins and not persisting to minor sins.

- Prevention from Eternal stay : This applies to disobedient monotheists according to the recurrent Hadith of intercession for the people of major sins. His saying: (who said there is no god but Allah Himself) means confirming the attributes of Allah besides restricted prevention from fire for the monotheists.

Sheikh Sulaiman bin Abdullah in this interpretation to this Hadith said: "Declaring that there is no god but Allah is a reason to enter the paradise and to escape the fire, but that will not be operative until all of its conditions are met and its bars are negated. Thus, Al Hassan when he was told that some people say: (Who says there is no god but Allah shall enter the paradise) he said: "who says there is no god but Allah and gives it its rights and conditions will enter the paradise".

Wahsb bin Munbih said to those who asked him: Isn't there is no god but Allah the key to paradise? He said: (yes but a key must have teeth to open)

This means that Allah tied entrance to the paradise with true faith and good deeds.

Abi Ayoub narrated that a man said: O the Messenger of Allah, tell me about a deed that qualifies me to enter the paradise, he said: "worship Allah without a partner, perform the prayers, give Zakah (Giving alms) and maintain the ties of kinship".

In Musnad, Bishr bin Khasaria said: I went to the Prophet (ABPBUH) to pledge allegiance to him. He stipulated to declare that there is no god but Allah, Muhammad is his servant Messenger, to perform the prayers, to give zakah (Giving alms), to perform Hajj (Pilgrimage to Makkah), to fast Ramadan and to fight for the cause of Allah. I said, two of these, I swear to Allah, I can't afford; Jihad and alms. The Prophet said while shaking my hand "if no Jihad (to strive by all means for Allah's sake) and no alms, how can you enter the paradise?" then I said, so Messenger of Allah I pledge to do all of them.

This Hadith indicates Jihad and the alms are of the conditions of entering paradise, besides monotheism, praying, performing Hajj and fasting. There are many Hadiths on this subject which include preventing fire from the people of complete monotheism and that the deeds shall not be acceptable unless they were genuinely to the Exalted Allah. (Taiseer Al Aziz Al Hamied 91)

The fourth condition: Veracity contrary to lying and preventing hypocrisy

The proof of veracity is the saying of Allah, the Exalted in the Book:

"*Alif Lam Mim (1) Do men think that they will be left along on saying, we believe and that they will not be tested. (2) We did those before them, and Allah will certainly know those who are true from those who are false (3)*". (Al Ankaut)

And His saying:

"*Of the people there are some who say: "we believe in Allah and the Last day; but they do not really believe. (8) Fain would they deceive Allah and those who believe, but they only deceive themselves and realize it not. (9) In their hearts is a disease, and Allah has increased their disease and grievous is the penalty they incur because they are false to themselves(10)*" (Al Baqarah)

In Sunna: It is established in the Sahihain that Muath bin Jabal, Allah may be pleased with him, said the Prophet (ABPBUH) said: "*who declares that there is no god but Allah, and Muhammad is the slave and Messenger of Allah, shall be prevented from fire*" (Tayseer Al Aziz Al Hameed: 91)

Al Baghawi in his Tafseer for the verses: said:

"*Alif Lam Mim (1) O men think that they will be left alone on saying" we believe and they will not be tested (2) we did test those before then, and Allah will certainly know those who are true from those who are false (3)*". (Al Ankabut)

He says: Allah will test men in their selves and properties to see who is faithful and who is hypocrite, (Tafseer Al Baghawi 3/460)

Sheikh bin Othaimeen said: Lust is ill will and it is worse than doubtfulness as the latter may be corrected with knowledge, but the former, there is no hope to correct it until Allah wills. The lustful knows the right, but he is not following it.

A doubtful matter: Is confusion between the rights and the untrue due to ignorance and it may be dispelled by certainty.

Lusts

Allah, the Exalted says: "*Fair in the eyes of men is the love of things they covert; women and songs; heaped up hoards of gold and silver, horses branded and wealth of cattle and well-trilled land*" (Ali Imran: 14)

Desire

It includes:
- Prohibited songs
- Arrogance
- Exposing beauty
- Vanity
- Association
- Fanaticism

Al Shaabi, Allah may bestow His mercy upon him said:

Desire goes down with the desirer

O Lord bring out the blackness of heart

O Lord purify my heart

O Lord enlighten my heart

Sheikh bin Othaimeen said, Allah made these things attractive to men in order to test the hearts of men and to know the true believers.

Inspect your heart

Allah the Exalted says: "*of the people there are some who say: "we believe in Allah and the Last Day" but they do not (really) believe*" (8- Al Baqarah)

This is notice from Allah that hypocrites show faith with words but their hearts hide polytheism deceiving Allah and the Believers. Allah, the Glorious says: "*in their hearts is a disease and Allah has increased their disease*".

Reward is of the same kind of deed.

This is their punishment in the earthly life. Allah, the Exalted says in Bani Israel: "*when they went wrong, Allah let their hearts go wrong for Allah guides not those who are rebellious transgressors*" (5- Al Saff)

And their punishment in the hereafter, Allah, the Exalted says: "*And grievous is the penalty they incur because they are false*" (10- Al Baqarah)

Allah tells about the hypocrites: "*The hypocrites they think they are over reaching Allah but he will over-reach them; when they stand up to prayer they stand without earnestness to be seen of men but little do the hold Allah in remembrance*"

(142- Al Nisa)

"*They are distracted in mind even in the midst of it being sincerely for neither one group nor for another whom Allah leaves straying never wilt thou find for him the way*". (143- Al Nisa)

Ibin Saadi says: Allah, the Exalted tells us about the hypocrites that they think Allah knows not about their deception, but Allah knows their deception, which will be reflected to them by humiliation and prevention.

Allah, the Exalted says: "*One day will the hypocrites' men and women say to the believers: wait for us! Let us borrow from your light! It will be said: "Turn ye back to your rear! Then seek a light, so a wall will be put up between them with a gate therein within it will be mercy throughout, and without it all alongside will be punishment. Those without will call out, were we not with you?"*

(Al Hadid: 13 – 14) 87

Allah says: *"When they stand up to prayer, they stand languidly, to be seen by the people".*

Among the qualities of the hypocrites, is that they stand up for prayer languidly, because their hearts are empty from willingness to Allah. They flatter people and mention Allah rarely. They are neither with the believers apparently and covertly, nor with the disbelievers apparently and covertly.

Thus He said: *"who deceives Allah, no path you will find for him".* It means there is no way to guide him and the believers in Allah are to the contrary, they perform their worship actively, frequently mention Allah and Allah guided them to the straight way (Ibin Saadi 1/429)

In Sunna: Anas narrated after Muath that the Prophet (ABPBUH) said: *"O Muath bin Jabal"* he said: Here you are O the Messenger of Allah, he said, *"Any one who declares faithfully that there is no god but Allah, and Muhammad is the Messenger of Allah, he will be prevented from fire"* he said: O Messenger of Allah can I convey this good news to them? He said: *"They will count on it"*

I say: we see the concurrence between the foresaid Hadith and the verses, that utterance of the testimonies should be combined with heartily belief.

Allah, the Exalted says: *"when the hypocrites come to you, they say, we bear witness that you are indeed the Messenger of Allah and Allah knows that you are indeed His*", and Allah bears witness that the hypocrites are indeed liars.

(Al Munnafiqun: 1)

The Hadith has further indications including; A scholar may favor some of his students with certain issues of knowledge if he fears that they will not understand them.

And, averting evils takes priority over procuring benefits which is ascribed to Sharia, but not to mind. Although a critical proof is established by the Quran and Sunna, many people are unaware of it and Allah is implored for help.

88

Heartily Asceticism

Sheikh Saleh bin Hamied, Allah may protect him, said on the Hadith:

"Be ascetic in what other people have they will like you"

Asceticism is abstract meaning, that if people act uprightly towards you, thanks to Allah, and if they act badly towards you, control your feelings. Thus, you live peacefully and you win the respect of people.

So long as you maintain your dignity, people will like you, and whenever you run after them they will be away from you.

This is the rule of Allah.

Lessons from the Two Holy Mosques

The fifth condition: Loving this word and its meaning with pleasure

The proof of love is His saying: *"Yet there are men who take for worship others besides Allah as equal with Allah they love them as they should love Allah but those of faith are overflowing in their love for Allah"* (165- Al Baqarah)

"O ye who believe! If any from among you turn back from his faith, soon will Allah produce a people whom He will love as they will love Him lowly with the believers mighty against the rejecters, fighting in the way of Allah and never afraid of he reproaches of such as find fault" (54- Al Maidah)

In Sunna, that is established in Sahih, that Anas, Allah may be pleased with him said, the Prophet (ABPBUH) said: "who has three qualities will find the sweetness of faith: that love of Allah and his Messenger are more to him than anything else, to be loved by Allah and to hate returning to polytheism after Allah saved him from it, just as he hates to be thrown away in fire". (Muslim – Al Iman book)

Loving this word may be achieved through two things;

First: Allocating worship to Allah alone.

Second: Rejecting polytheism

The compiled book says: The origin and base of religion are two things:

First: Ordering worship to Allah alone charging who abandons Him with paganism.

Second: warning from joining a partner with Allah in worshipping Him and accusing the doer with paganism.

(First message on monotheism of the five messages of Shaikh Abdul Rahman bin

Hassan at Al Jami Al Fareed).

Consider His saying: *"yet there are men who take (for worship) others besides Allah"*

This verse confirms the oneness of Allah and assigning worship to Him alone. However, some people take equals to Allah.

And the meaning of His saying: *"But those of faith are overflowing in their love of Allah"* it means more love to Allah than the polytheists, because their love devoted to Allah alone, but the love of polytheists is joining others with Allah.

And His saying *"who renounces his religion"*

This is a statement from the Exalted Allah that Allah protected his religion and if some people renounce it, others will come to protect it who posses five features:

First: Allah loves them for their persistence in His religion and they love Allah by following His orders and avoiding His prohibitions.

Second: They are mild to the people of faith.

Third: Allah, the Exalted says: "Muhammad is the Messenger of Allah; and those who are with him are strong against unbelievers, but compassionate amongst each other" (29- Al Fath)

Fourth: They fight the polytheists to evaluate the word of Allah.

Fifth: *"Never be afraid of the blame of anyone who blames"*. They say the truth wherever they are according to the direction of Sharia. The promise of Allah in this verse was fulfilled at the hands of Abi Bakr and his army when they fought the renouncers following death of the Messenger of Allah until they brought them back to the realm of Islam.

The verses indicate:

Al Nawawi commented on the Hadith *"who possesses three attributes -"* This is a great Hadith and one of the principles of Islam.

The religious scholars say that sweetness of faith means deriving pleasure from obedience and bearing hardships in the pathway of satisfaction of Allah and His Messenger (ABPBUH).

And preferring this to the vain again of the earthly life, loving the Exalted Allah and His Messenger (ABPBUH).

Al Qadhi, Allah may bestow His mercy upon him, said that who feels the sweetness of faith, is the man who accepts Allah as His Lord and Muhammad (ABPBBUH) as Messenger of Allah with real affection and certain belief.

Some religion scholars said: Love is connivance of heart to what pleases Allah, by loving what He loves and repelling what He hates (Muslim at Sharh Al Nawawi 2/3)

Thus, the sweetness of faith is completed with three things.

First

Devotion of worship to Allah

Second

Affirming love from Allah side and the man side

Third

Allah praises the people of faith for their perfect love to Him

Fourth

The good result is for the people of faith

Love of Allah and His Messenger more than anything else.

Repelling the contrasts of faith just like repelling to be thrown in fire.

Obedience to Allah and His Messenger by doing what they like and avoiding what they hate.

This includes refutation to what some people believe that who is born a Muslim, is favored to who was polytheist then he became Muslim.

Anas, Allah may be pleased with him said that he asked the Prophet: when is the Judgement Day?

He said: what did you prepare for it -----------

The best comments on the Hadith are two:

First: Al Baidhawi said: dual in the Hadith means that each disobedience is independent which is eloquent reply.

Second: Al Khatib comment "just like to be thrown in Fire" equals between going back to polytheism and being thrown in Fire.

I said the Hadith tells that Allah is loved by the faithful and He loves them.

And it includes refutation to the exaggerators who imagine that a sin committed by a man is absolute blemish, but truth is that it is blemish if he did not repent. Therefore, the immigrants and the helpers were the best of this nation, although they were polytheists worshipping idols at the beginning. Who is shifted from astray to guidance and from sins to good deeds, his reward will be doubled.

Shaikhul Islam said.

It also includes enmity to the polytheists, because who hates an attribute hates its holder and since polytheism is hated the polytheists will be hated.

(Tayseer Al Aziz Al Hameed 477)

The sixth condition: Submission to its rights

This means the required deeds, in faith to Allah and in quest for His satisfaction. The proof of submission is His saying: *"Turn ye to your Lord in repentance and bow to his will"*. (54- Al Zumar) and *"Who can be better in religion than one who submits his whole self to Allah"* (125- Al Nisa) and *"Whoever submits his whole self to Allah and is a doer of good has grasped indeed the most trustworthy handhold and with Allah rest the end"* (22- Luqman) and *"But no by the Lord they can have not real faith until they make thee judge in all disputes between them and find in their souls no resistance against thy dedision by accept them with the fullest conviction"* (65- Al Nisa)

In Sunna: The Hadith: *"No one of you will be faithful until his own way is in compliance with what I brought"* (Al Baghawu – Sharh Al Sunna 1/2/3)

In the verse: *"Turn ye to your Lord and bow to his will before the punishment comes on you after that ye shall not be helped".* (54: Al Zumar)

Al Baghawi said; it means turn back to your Lord with obedience and sincere monotheism, before the punishment comes on you and you shall not be helped.

Ibin Saadi says: For what, Allah commanded to turn to Him and subjecting hearts and organs to Him and *"bow to his will"* is indication to loyalty, as the deeds without loyalty shall be fruitless. If it is asked what is turn and submission, Allah, the exalted, answers: *"Follow the revelation given unto you from your Lord"*

(3- Al Araf)

(Tafseer Ibin Saadi 4/332)

I said: The interpretation of these two Imams is concluded from the connection between this verse and the verse before: *"Say: O my servants who have transgressed against their souls despair not of the mercy of Allah for Allah forgives all sins for He is soft-forgiving most merciful"* (53- Al Zumar)

The Hadith and the verse, both urge for turn to Allah, the Exalted, the Glorious.

Allah, the Exalted says: *"who can be better in religion than one who submits his whole self to Allah, does good, and follows the way for Ibrahim the true in Allah?"* (125- Al Nisa)

This means that no better piety and worshipping than that who combined in his words and acts between Islam and good deeds which means that he possessed loyalty to Allah and followed the steps of his Messenger (ABPBUH).

Al Hafith bin Katheer said: penalty for sins may be either in the earthly life, which is better for the doer, or in the hereafter.

We ask pardon of Allah the Generous, the Merciful Who will not decrease any of the good deed of men and women as much as a pit of a date stone.

In His saying:

"who can be better in religion than one who submits to Allah, does good". It means devoting the deeds to Allah and following what the Messenger revealed. No deed will be good without these two conditions, to be dedicated genuinely to Allah and to be in compliance with the commands of Allah. If any of these two conditions is missed the deed will be unsound. If loyalty was missed, the deed will be hypocrisy, and if compliance was missed he will be astray. "Such are they from whom we shall accept the best of their deeds and pass by their ill deeds they shall be among the companions of he garden". (16- Al Ahqaf)

Allah, the Exalted says: *"So we have taught thee the inspired message follow the ways of Ibrahim the true in faith and joined not gods with Allah"*

(123- Al Nahl)

True in faith means turning away from polytheism mindfully and turning to right completely and insistently. (Tafseer Ibin Katheer 1/573)

In brief, the verse includes two things:

First: No deed will be accepted by Allah, unless it combines belief in Allah, loyalty to Him and following His Messenger (ABPBUH) which is the end of submission.

Second: The true religion revealed to Muhammad (ABPBUH) is the religion of Ibrahim (Allah's beloved). Allah says: "Whoever submits his whole self to Allah and is a doer of good has grasped indeed the most trustworthy handhold and with Allah rest the end". (22- Luqman)

The Exalted Allah, tells that the way to the most trustworthy handhold is subjection to Allah supplemented with good deeds.

In support of this meaning, we convey what Ibin Katheer said on this verse: *"Whoever rejects evil and believes in Allah hath grasped the most trustworthy handhold that never breaks and Allah heareth and knoweth all things"* (256- Al Baqarah)

It means that who casts away equals and idols he had held the most trustworthy handhold, and had followed the straight way.

Mujahid said: *"The trustworthy handhold"* means faith

Al Saadi said: It means Islam

Saeed bin Jubair and Dhahaak Said: it means there is no god but Allah.

Anas bin Malik said: the trustworthy handhold means the Quran.

Salem Abi Al Jaad said: it is loving what Allah loves and hating what Allah dislikes.

All these sayings are true and there is no contradiction between them (Ibin Katheeer 1/319)

The verse: *"But no by the Lord, they can have no real faith"* Allah, the Exalted, informs that the apparent and the hidden faith is achieved through three conditions.

First: Recourse upon the judgement of the Prophet himself in his life and upon his method after his death.

Second: Acceptance of such judgements with open hearts.

Third: Complete subjection to his judgement (ABPBUH).

The meaning of this verse is clarified by the Hadith narrated by Bukhari- in Al Tafsseer Book that Orwa bin Al Zubair said: (Al Zubair disputed with a man from Al Ansar on irrigating a land, the Prophet said: «0 Zubair, irrigate then allow water to your neighbour». Al Ansari said, 0 Messenger of Allah, for he is your cousin? The Prophet was agitated and said: «Irrigate Zubair and retain water until it comes to the wall, then send the water to your neighbour». Zubair said, I think these verses were revealed for such cases: «But no by the Lord they can have no real faith until they make thee judge in all disputes between them» (65- Al Nisa)

The matching verse in subjection to the judgement of Allah and His Messenger:

«If ye differ in anything among yourselves refer it to Allah and his Messenger».

(59- Al Nisa)

Sheikh Abdul Rahman bin Saadi, Allah may bestow His mercy upon him, said on discussing this verse and the verses before, that all disputes among people on religious matters to be referred to Allah and His Messenger, that is to the Quran and Sunna where in them decision on all disputed matters either expressly or overtly, or generally by application to similar matters.

Because the Book of Allah and the Sunna of His Messenger are the foundation of the religion and faith will not be straight without them, which is a condition for faith «If you believe in Allah and the Last Day».

This means: referring to Allah and to His Messenger «is the best for you and has the best outcome» (Tafseer Ibin Saadi 1/362).

What the verses tell:

First: Necessity of loyalty to Allah alone and necessity of following the Messenger (ABPBUH) are the way to the most trustworthy handhold.

Second: Submission to the judgement of Allah and His Messenger apparently and covertly are obligatory.

The proof is the Prophet saying: (No one of you will be faithful until his way is according to what I brought).

Allah, the Exalted says: «But no by the Lord they can have no real faith until they make thee judge in all disputes between them and find in their souls no resistance against thy decisions but accept them with the fullest conviction». (65- Al Nisa)

And Allah the Exalted said: «It is not for a believing man or woman, when a matter has been decided by Allah and his Messenger to have any choice in the matter» (36- Al Ahzab)

Allah, the Exalted, condemned who hates what He likes and who likes what He hated.

Allah, the Exalted, says: «That is because they hate the revelation of Allah, so he has made their deeds fruitless» (9- Muhammad)

Thus, every believer shall be obliged to like what Allah likes by performing his duties, and to hate what Allah hates by avoiding what He prohibited.

It is established in Sahihain that the Prophet (ABPBUH) said: «No one-of you will be a believer until I am adored to him more than himself, and more than his children, family and all people».

(Jami Al Gloom Wal Hikam 364)

I said: It seems to me, and Allah knows best, the compiler quoted the Hadith on basis of the soundness of its meaning as Al Hafith bin Rajab stated, supported with proofs.

The seventh condition: Unobjectionable Acceptance

The proof for acceptance is the saying of Allah, the Exalted:

«Just in the same way whenever we sent a warner before thee to any people the wealthy ones among them said we found our fathers following a certain religion and we will certainly follow in their footsteps». (23- Al Zukhruf)

«what even if I brought you better guidance than that which you found your fathers following?» (24- Al Zukhruf) Do you follow me « They said for us we deny that ye Prophets are sent» (24- Al Zukhruf)

He knows that they will not follow the righteous way, but they intend to follow the false. «now see what was the end of those who rejected» (25- Al Zukhruf)

And He says: «For they when they were told that there is no god except Allah would puff themselves up with pride» (35- Al Saffat)

«And say what shall we give up our gods for the sake of a poet possessed»

(36Al Saffat)

In Sunna, it is established that Abu Musa, Allah may be pleased with him, narrated that the Prophet (ABPBUH) said: «the example of guidance and knowledge with which Allah sent me is like abundant rain falling on earth, a part of which was fertile that absorbed the rain water and brought forth abundant vegetation and grass. And another part was hard and held water that Allah benefited the people with it for drinking and cultivation. And a part was barren land which could neither hold water nor bring forth grass. The first is the example for the person who comprehends Allah's Religion (Islam) and gets benefit from the knowledge, which Allah revealed through me and learns and teaches it to others. The last example is for a person who does not care for it and does not take Allah's guidance revealed through me.

(Sahih Al Bukhari, the Book of knowledge, chapter, merit of who learns and teaches)

Allah, the Exalted says: «Just in the same way whenever we sent a warner before thee to any people the wealthy ones among them said we found our fathers' following a certain religion and we will certainly follow in their footsteps».

(23- Al Zukhruf)

Allah, the Glorious, tells that Quraish in rejecting the mission of the Messenger (ABPBUH) is similar to the deed of the old nations with their Prophets.

Sheikh Abdul Rahman Al Saadi commented on this verse that the wealthy people who were lured by the worldly life said: « we found our fathers following a certain religion and we will certainly follow in their footsteps». (23- Al Zukhruf)

Such argument by this astray polytheist group in imitating their astray forefathers was merely fanaticism and null uncertainty.

«what even if I brought you better guidance than that which you found your fathers following?» (24- Al Zukhruf)

Do you follow me « They said for us we deny that ye Prophets are sent » (24- Al Zukhruf)

He knows that they will not follow the righteous way, but they intend to follow the false. «now see what was the end of those who rejected » (25- Al Zukhruf)

Those must know that if they continue their denying, they will incur what they have already incurred.

(Tafseer Ibin Saadi 4/442)

What the verses tell:

First: Firming up the heart of the Prophet (ABPBUH) and consoling him, that what he says is not heresy and his people are not liers.

Second: Warning against disobeying the Prophet (ABPBUH)

Third: Imitation is unsafe and it is the greatest means that turn away from accepting the right and guidance. What indicates that is established in the Sahihain after Saeed bin Al Musaieb after his father, that when Abu Talib was dying, the Prophet (ABPBUH) came in and he found there Aba Jahl and Abdulla bin Al Mughira and he said: «would you like to abandon the creed of Abdul Muttalib to implore Allah to forgive you». Then the verse came «It is not fitting for the Prophet and those who believe that they should pray for forgiveness » (113- Al Tawbah)

And Allah, the Exalted said: «It is true thou wilt not be able to guide everyone whom thou lovest but Allah guides those whom He will » (56- Al Qasas)

The compiler said on the 8th matter (Muslim / Al Tawheed Book) Harm of the People of Evils on Man.

The 9th matter: Disadvantage of glorification of ancestors and masters

Consider how Abu Talib preferred the faith of his ancestors and refused to declare the righteous testimony

«verily in this is a message for any that has a heart and understanding or who gives ear and earnestly witnesses (the truth)» (37- Qat)

Beware, 0 Muslims, of unwise fanaticism and blind imitation.

Allah, the Exalted says: «For they when they were told that there is no god except Allah, would puff themselves up with pride. And say: «what! Shall we give up our gods for the sake of a poet possessed?» (35-36 Al Saffat)

They did not only turn away from his call, but they described him as possessed poet although they know he is not a poet, but he is the greatest of the creatures of Allah (Tafseen Ibin Saadi 4/256)

I said: Then the following verse came to refute the allegations of the atheists:

«Nay! He has come with the very truth and he confirms the message of the Messengers before him» (37- Al Saftat)

Al Hafith bin Katheer said: Allah the Exalted replied to them that he has come with the very truth and he confirms the messages of the previous Messengers «Nothing is said to thee that was not said to the Messengers before you» (43 Fussilat)

(Tafseer Ibin Katheer 417)

Al Nawawi, Allah may bestow His mercy upon him said: (The meaning of the Hadith is exemplifying the true religion he brought as rain and three types of land as well as people:

The first type: Is the land that benefits from rain and grows grass and plants similarly to the people who learn the true religion and teach it to other people.

The second type: Is the land that holds water without benefit for itself but there is benefit for people. The second type of people is the same, they have good memories, but without sharp minds. They keep their knowledge until acknowledge seeker comes to them to take his need.

The third type of land: Is the barren land, which gives no grass and keeps no water to benefit the people.

The third type of people is similar; they have no preserving hearts and no clear minds. If they receive knowledge, they neither make benefit of it, nor keep it for others to benefit.

This Hadith shows various types of knowledge:

Exemplifying, learning and teaching, urging for learning and teaching and condemnation of turning away from seeking knowledge. His word ended Allah may protect him and Allah knows best.

Chapter Five
Nullifiers of Islam

Nullifiers of Islam

Sheikh Muhammad bin Abdul Wahab, Allah may bestow His mercy upon him, said; know that the nullifications of Islam are ten:

First: Joining a partner with Allah.

Allah, the Exalted says: «Allah forgives not that partners should be set up with Him; but He forgives anything else, to whom He pleases» (48- Al Nisa)

And He says: «Whoever joins other gods with Allah, Allah will forbid him the garden, and the fire will be his abode». (72- Al Maidah)

This includes asking help from dead people, making vow and slaughtering for them.

Second: Who sets up mediators between himself and Allah, asking them for intercession and relies on them is considered unanimously atheist.

Allah, the Exalted says: «we only serve them in order that they may bring us nearer to Allah» (3- Al Zumar)

Third: Who will not judge a polytheist as disbeliever, doubt his polytheism or correct his creed is pagan. Allah the Exalted says: «0 ye who believe! Take not my enemies and yours as friends or protectors offering them your love»

(1- Al Mumtahinah)

Fourth: Who believes that a method other than that of the Prophet (ABPBUH) is better, as those who prefer the judgement of tyrants to his judgement, is pagan.

Allah, the Exalted says: «But no by the Lord they can have no real faith until they make thee judge in all disputes between them and find in their souls no resistance against thy decisions but accept them with the fullest conviction» (65- Al Nisa)

Fifth: Who hates anything brought by the Messenger (ABPBUH) even though he performed it, is pagan.

Allah the Exalted says: «That is because they hate the revelation of Allah; so He has made their deeds fruitless» (9- Muhammad)

Sixth: Who mocks at anything of the religion of the Messenger (ABPBUH) or his reward or punishment is pagan. The proof is His saying: «If thou dost question them, they declare with emphasis we were only talking idly and in play. Say; was it at Allah, and his signs and his Messenger that ye were mocking»

(65- Al Tawbah)

Seventh: Magic including diverting love or bringing love. Who practices or accepts it is pagan. The proof is His saying: «But neither of these taught anyone without saying: «we are not only for trial: so do not blaspheme» (102- Al Baqarah)

Eighth: Supporting polytheists against Muslims. The proof is His saying:

«And he amongst you that turns to them for friendship is of them verily Allah guideth not a people unjust». (51- Al Maidah)

Ninth: Who quits the religion of Muhammad (ABPBUH) is pagan. Allah the Exalted says:

«If anyone desires a religion other than Islam submission to Allah never will it be accepted of him; and in the hereafter he will be in the ranks of those who have lost all spiritual good» (85- Al Imran)

Tenth: Turning away from the religion of Allah, not learning it and not applying it.

« Allah the Exalted says: «And who does more wrong than one to whom are recited the signs of his Lord and who then turns away there from? Verily from those who transgress we shall exact due retribution». (22- Al Sajdah)

There is no difference in these nullifications among mocker, serious and afraid except the compelled. They are all very risky and more probable to occur. A Muslim should be aware of these and should protect himself from them. We take refuge with Allah from His anger and painful punishment.
.

His word ended, may Allah be merciful to him.

Chapter Six
The truth of the testification that Muhammad is the Messenger of Allah

Sheikh Abdul Aziz Al Shaikh, Allah may protect him, says in his book; the reality of testimony «Muhammad is the Messenger of Allah (ABPBUH)

A chapter on the Prophet's lineage

Allah, the Exalted, says: «Allah did confer a great favor on the believes when he sent among them a Messenger from among themselves rehearsing unto them the signs of Allah sanctifying them, and instructing them in scripture and wisdom,

while before that they had been in manifest error». (164- Al Imran)

In Sahih Muslim, Wathila bin Al Asqa, Allah may be pleased with him, narrated that he heard the Messenger of Allah saying: «Allah chose Kanana from the offspring of Ismail, chose Quraish from Kanana, chose Bani Hashim from Quraish and chose me from Bani Hashim» Hadith No. 2276

In Sahihain (Bukhari and Muslim) Hadith No. 1373:

Abi Sufian narrated that Hercules asked him about the lineage of the Prophet (ABPPBUH). Abi Sufian replied that he is of noble lineage. Hercules replied that Messsengers are sent from the elite of their people. Thus, the Prophet Muhammad is of noble lineage. He is Muhammad bin Abdullah bin Abdul Muttalib bin Hashim bin Abd Munaf bin Qusai bin Murra bin Adnan.

His lineage is known well, agreed upon by genealogists and Adnan is offspring of Ismail the Prophet of Allah, and Ismail is the son of Ibrahim, peace be upon him.

The mother of the Prophet is Amina, daughter of Wahb bin Abd Munaf bin Zahra bin Kulab and his father meets with his mother in their grandfather Kulab bin Murra. Wahab, the father of his mother was the chief of Bani Zahra. Thus, the Prophet combined the noble ancestry from his father and from his mother.

Chapter on his birth

The Prophet was born in the year of the Elephant without disagreement among the historians. His birth: verily, he was born on Monday as he said, when he was asked about fasting on Monday, he said: «on this day, I was born, on it I was sent and on this day it was revealed to me» (Reported by Muslim 1/819) Hadith No. 1162/196).

As for the month of birth there was disagreement on it:

It was said: on 12th Rabi I

And it was said: on 8th of Rabi I

 And it was said: in Ramadan

And it was said: on 27th of Rajab which is the most unlikely

Chapter on his mission (ABPBUH)

He was inspired when he was forty years of age and the beginning of revelation happened when he was contemplating in the cave of Hira, then Gabriel came to him and said: «read»

Aisha, the mother of faithful believers narrated: The commencement of the Divine inspiration to Allah's Messenger was in the form of righteous dreams which came true like bright day light, and then the love of seclusion was bestowed upon him. He used to go in seclusion in the cave of Hira where he used to worship (Allah alone) continuously for many nights before returning to his family. He used to take with him the journey food for the stay and then came back to his wife Khadija to take his food likewise again until suddenly the truth descended upon him while he was in the Cave of Hira. The angel came to him and asked him to read. The Prophet replied «I do not know how to read». The Prophet added «Then the angel caught me (forcefully) and pressed me so hard that I could not bear it any more. He then released me and asked me again to read.

Thereupon he caught me again and pressed me a second time. He then released me and asked me to read but again I replied «I do not know how to read (or what shall I read)? Then he said «Read in the name of your Lord, who has created. Has created man from a clot. Read! And your Lord is the Most Generous». Then Allah's Messenger returned with the inspiration and with his heart beating severely. Then he went to Khadija bint Khuwailid and said «cover me, cover me». They covered him until his fear was over and after that he told Khadija everything that had happened and he said, «I fear that something may happen to me» Khadija,

Allah may be pleased with her, replied, «Never! By Allah, Allah will never disgrace you. You keep good relations with your kith and kin, help the poor and the destitute, serve your quests generously and assist the deserving calamity - afflicted ones». Khadija then accompanied him to her cousin Waraqa bin Naufal bin Asad, who during the period of ignorance became a Christian and used to write in Hebrew letters. He could write from the Gospel in Hebrew as much as Allah wished him to write. He was an old man and had lost his eyesight. Khadija said to him :

«0 my cousin! Listen to the story of your nephew» Waraqa asked, «0 my nephew! What have you seen?

«Allah's Messenger described whatever he had seen. Waraqa said, «This is the same one (who keeps the secrets i.e. angel Gabriel whom Allah sent to Mosa. I wish I were young and could live up to the time when your people would turn you out. Allah's Messenger asked, «will they drive me out?» He replied in the affirmative and said, «Anyone who came with something similar to what you have brought, was treated with hostility, and if I should remain alive till the day (when you will be turned out) then I would support you strongly». But after few days Waraqa died and the divine inspiration was also paused for a while. (Reported by Al Bukhari - Sahih Al Bukhari 1/2-4)

Chapter on his death

Allah, the Exalted says addressing His Prophet: «Truly thou wilt die and truly they will die» (30- Al Zumar)

And He says: «Muhammad is no more than a Messenger; many were the Messengers that passed away before him. If he died or were slain, will ye then turn back on your heels» (144- Ali Imran)

And He says: «We granted not to any man before thee permanent life here; if then thou shouldst die, would they live permanently» (34- Al Anbiya)

The Prophet died after he rendered the trust, announced the message of his Allah and fought truly for the cause of Allah.

«This day have those who reject faith given up all hope of your religion yet fear them not but fear me. This day have I perfected your religion for you completed my favour upon you and have chosen for you Islam as your religion»

(3- Al Maidah)

Allah, the Exalted, announced the death of His Prophet when he revealed to him the Sura of Al Nasr. In Sahih Al Bukhari, after Ibin Abbas, Allah may be pleased with them narrated that Omar said: what do you say in Allah's saying «When comes the help of Allah and victory» (1- Al Nasr), I said, it is the term of life of the Messenger of Allah. (Sahih Al Bukhari 6/94)

Abi Saeed Al Khadri, narrated that the Messenger of Allah sat on the pulpit and said; «A man was offered by Allah the option between the splendor of life and what Allah has, and he opted what Allah has» Death of the Prophet was similar to death of all men, started with stupor, then the soul left the body and his body became flaccid.

Ibin Abbas, Allah may be pleased with them said; (The Prophet went out in his last sickness tying his head with a piece of cloth). (Sahih Al Bukhari 1/120)

Muslim narrated that Iundub said: This sermon was 5 days before his death. (Sahhih Muslim 1/377 - Hadith No. 532)

(Aisha, Allah may be pleased with her said: One of the blessings of Allah is that the Prophet died at my home, in my day --)

Reported by Al Bukhari (Sahih Al Bukhari 5/141, 142)

His death was on Monday, according to Aisha as reported by Al Bukhari in his Sahhih. He died in the eleventh year of Hijra (Immigration) and in the month of Rabi I when he was sixty three years of age according to the group of his companions.

During the period between his mission until his death, great events happened. He called for the path of Allah, endured pain, fought and immigrated until Allah decreed victory for him and for his companions. When he passed away he had conveyed the message of his Lord and his religion is lasting forever.

His religion is protected and prevailing all creeds. His people, who are completing it will be victorious.

Allah, the Exalted says: «Already has our word been passed before this to our servants sent by us» (171- Al Saffat)

«That they would certainly be assisted» (172- Al Saffat)

«And that our forces they surely must conquer» (173- Al Saffat)

And He says: «It is He who hath sent his Messenger with guidance and the religion of truth to proclaim it over all religion even though the pagans may detest

it». (33- Al Tawbah)

Following his way in backing the religion of Allah, endurance of pain for that, following his way in fighting the enemies of Allah. All these matters should be taken as examples from the perfect creature, the master of men and the best absolutely.

This is just a small portion of the autobiography of this great Prophet and this brief message is just to draw attention to the fact that Muhammad is the Messenger of Allah and every Muslim must complete and apply his way in order to avoid the punishment of Allah.

Allah may preserve us and all Muslim brothers from the causes of Allah's anger and we implore Allah to cover us with His mercy, He is Generous and Most Noble.

Chapter on his attributes

The names of the Prophet indicate great meanings.

Allah, the Exalted called his name (Muhammad) saying: «Muhammad is the Messenger of Allah; and those who are with him are strong against unbelievers but compassionate amongst each other» (29- Al Fath)

And He says: «Muhammad is not the father of any of your men but he is the Messenger of Allah and the seal of the Prophets» (40- Al Ahzab)

And Allah, the Exalted says: «But those who believe and work deeds of righteousness, and believe in the revelation sent down to Muhammad for it is the truth from their Lord, He will remove from them their ills and improve their condition»

(2- Muhammad)

And Allah, the Exalted says: «Muhammad is no more than a Messenger; many were the Messengers that passed away before him. If he died or were slain, will ye then turn back on your heels, if any did turn back on his heels, not the least harm will he do to Allah; but Allah on the other hand will swiftly reward those who serve him with gratitude» (144- Ali Imran)

Hassan bin Thabit, Allah may be pleased with him, said this line of poetry:

He derived from his name to dignify him

The throne Lord is laudable and this is Muhammad

This line is originally for Abi Talib, Hassan quoted it in his poem.

From his name, also, Ahmad, which Essa mentioned in his glad tidings about the mission of the Prophet. Allah, the Exalted says: «And giving glad tidings of a Messenger to come after me whose name shall be Ahmad» (6- Al Saff)

Of his names, also, (Al Mutawakkil) i.e. relying on Allah,

Abdulla bin Amro bin Al Aas narrated about the attributes of the Prophet in Torrah» you are my servant and Messenger, called you Al Mutawakkil» (Reported by Al Bukhari).

Among the names of the Prophet, Jubair bin Mataam narrated that the Prophet said: «I have names: I am Muhammad, Ahmad, Al Mahi (Allah eliminates polytheism through me, I am Al Hashir (Gatherer) and I am Al Aqip (the last Messsenger)» Sahih Al Bukhari 4/162 and 6/62 and Sahih Muslim 4/1828 Hadith No. 2354 (Agreed upon).

Abi Musa Al Ashari, Allah may be pleased with him said: «The Messenger of Allah called himself names, some of them we memorize and some we do not, he said: «I am Muhammad, Ahmad, follower, gatherer, Prophet of repentance and Prophet of mercy» (Sahih Muslim 4/1828, Hadith No. 2355) Reported by Muslim.

The meaning of Muhammad is derived from praise, which includes praise and esteem of the subject. Derivation of passive participle denotes recurrence of the verb (Explanatin of Mashhour bin Hassan Salman, page 277).

As for the other names they were explained in the narration of Jubair bin Mataam above.

Muhammad is the Messenger of Allah

Differentiated between the righteous and the impious

Through him showed the right way

Correct

blurring

sight

Through him Allah guided the people

Gatherer for all creatures

Compassionate with the

believers

Saved people from darkness

Allah, the Exalted says: « Now hath come unto you a Messenger from amongst yourselves it grieves him that ye should perish ardently anxious is he over your to the believers is he most kind and merciful» (128- Al Tawbah)

Guided out from astray

Chapter on his qualities

The Prophet is the master of men.

Abdullah bin Salam, Allah may be pleased with him, narrated that the Prophet said: «I am master of Adam's children, without pride». (Sahih Ibin Habban Haddith No. 6242, 6475)

Abi Hurairah narrated the same Hadith differently «I am master of Adam's children on the Day of Judgement, the first to be resurrected, the first intercessor and the first interceded». (Sahih Muslim 4/1782) Hadith No. 2278.

Al Izz said: The master is who holds noble qualities and lofty ethics that make him the best in the earthly life and in the hereafter.

The Prophet said: «I am master of Adam's children without pride»: So that his people will Know his rank with Allah, the Exalted. And to stop the false illusion of the ignorant, he said «without pride» (The book of the scholar Aliz bin Abdul Aziz Al Salami - Bidayat Al Sool page 34).

Ibin Umar said: «The people on the Day of Judgement gather in groups, each group follows its Prophet and they ask for intercession until it reaches the Prophet and that is the praiseworthy station» Reported by Bukhari (Sahih Al Bukhari 5/228).

Abdullah bin Amro narrated that he heard the Prophet saying: «when you hear the Muezzin(Who calls for prayer) say as he says, then bestow blessings on me, who asks for it once, Allah, bestows ten on him, then ask for a status for me in the garden, it is a status for one of the servants of Allah, I hope to be that one, and who asks (wasila) for me shall be entitled to intercession». (Sahih Muslim Hadith No. 384, reported by Muslim).

Amongst his attributes, not to be called in his abstract name as Allah called him in his best names and attributes «O Prophet» and «O Messenger» which is not established to the other Prophets who were called by their names:

« O Adam! Dwell» Al Baqarah: 35

«O Essa the son of Mary Recount my favor» Al Maidah: 110

«O Mosa! Verily I am Allah» Al Qasas: 30

«O Nouh come down with peace» Hud: 48

«O Ibrahim» Al Saffat: 104

«O Lut! We are Messengers from thy Lord» Hud: 81

Allah, the Exalted, prohibited His creatures to call him by his abstract name:

«Deem not the summons of the Messenger among yourselves like the summons of one of you to another» (63- Al Nur)

Amongst his attributes is that the miracles of all Prophets disappeared, but the miracle of the master of men, the Quran, is existing forever.

Allah, the Exalted says: «We have without doubt sent down the message and we will assuredly guard it» (9- Al Hijr)

Jabir bin Abdullah Al Ansari narrated that the Prophet said: «I was given five things no one before got them: every

Prophet was sent to his people in particular, but I was sent to all mankind, I was allowed the booties, while no one before was allowed to have them, the good earth was allowed to me for prayer, whenever the time of prayer comes you can pray wherever you are, I was saved from terror and I was given intercession» (Sahih Al Bukhari 1/86 and Sahih Muslim 1/370, 371, Hadith No. 521)

Chapter on his morals

Allah, the Exalted says: «And thou on an exalted standard of character»

(4-AI Qalam)

Saad bin Hisham bin Amer said: I went to Aisha, Allah may be pleased with her, and said: O mother of believers, tell me about the ethics of the Messenger of Allah. She said: His morals were the Quran , consider Allah, the Exalted, saying «And thou on an exalted standard of character». I said, I wanted to devote myself to worship Allah. She said: Do not do that, consider «you have indeed in the Messenger of Allah a beautiful pattern of conduct» (21- Al Ahzab)

The Messenger of Allah was married and was provided with children.

Allah, the Exalted, perfected his creation since childhood and before the mission. He never worshiped an idol, never drank alcohol, never committed any offence and he was called among his people the «truthful and trustworthy».

Jabir bin Abdullah said: «when the Kaabah was built, the Prophet and Al Abbas were moving stones» (Sahih Al Bukhari - Hadith No. 340 and Sahih Muslim).

Allah, the Exalted, mentioned some of his morals. He says:

«It is a part of the mercy of Allah that thou dost deal gently with them»

(159Ali Imran)

And, the Exalted says: «Muhammad is the Messenger of Allah and those who are with him are strong against unbelievers, but compassionate amongst each other» (29-Al Fath)

And, the Exalted says, «Now hath come unto you a Messenger from amongst yourselves it grieves him that ye should perish ardently anxious is he over your to the believers is he most kind and merciful» (128- Al Tawbah)

And He said: «We sent thee not but as a mercy for all creatures»

(107- Al Anbiya)

Narrated by Sahih Al Bukhari that Ataa bin Yasar said: I met Abdullah bin Amro bin Al Aas and I said: tell me about the attribute of the Prophet in Torah, he said: by Lord, he is described in Torah with some of his attributes in Quran: o Prophet: truly we have sent you as a witness, a bearer of glad tidings and a warner».

Aisha, Allah may be pleased with her, narrated: whenever Allah's Messenger was given a choice of one of two matters, he would choose the easier of the two as long as it was not sinful, but if it was sinful he would not approach it Allah's Messenger never took revenge for his own sake, but when Allah's laws were breached he would take revenge for Allah's sake.

From the manners of the Prophet also, his modesty and kidding with children. Anas, Allah may be pleased with him, said: the Prophet was the kindest in his manners. I had a weaned brother and when the Prophet saw him, he said: Aba Omair, what did the little birdy do? And he was playing with him».

(Agreed upon in Sahih Al Bukhari and Sahih Muslim, Hadith No. 2150)

Chapter on his congenital qualities

Our Prophet, Allah the Exalted, perfected his creation and provided him with the best image and the most perfect morals.

Considering the congenital qualities of the Prophet provides the believer with certain benefits including:

- The more, the Muslim knows about his Prophet's qualities, the more he will like him and his faith will be stronger.

- Anas narrated that the Prophet said: «Whoever sees me in a dream then he has seen me indeed, satan cannot appear in my shape and the dream of a righteous man is one of forty-six parts of Prophethood».

(Sahih Al Bukhari and Sahih Muslim - Hadith No. 2266)

- Narrated Al-Bara bin Azib: The Prophet was of moderate height having broad shoulders, hair reaching his ear-lobes, I saw him in a red cloak and I had never seen a more handsome person than him. (Sahih Al Bukhari 4/165).

Anas bin Malik said: The Prophet was of medium height amongst the people, neither tall nor short, he had a rosy color neither absolutely white nor deep brown, his hair was neither completely curly nor quite lank, divine inspiration was revealed to him when he was forty years old. He stayed ten years in Makka receiving the divine inspiration and stayed in Al Madina ten more years when he expired, he had scarcely twenty white hairs in his head and beard» (Hadith No. 1580).

Ali bin Abi Talib, Allah may be pleased with him said: «The Prophet was of medium height, with large hands, bulky head, stouty bones, with long chest hair, when he walks as if he is walking on a slope of land, I never saw like him before or after» (Sunan Al Tarmathi 5/598 - Hadith No. 3637 - reported by Tarmathi and he said: Good Hadith)

Zamakhshari said in his book «Al Faieq»: Bulky hands is praise to men and it means patience and power.

(Dar Al Fikr print 3/377).

Chapter on the reality of the testimony of Muhammad is the Messenger of Allah supported with proofs

The reality of the testimony of Muhammad is the Messenger of Allah includes several matters on top of which is faith, complete faith that Muhammad is indeed the Messenger of Allah «Muhammad is the Messenger of Allah» (29- Al Fath)

And his mission is universal for all races. Allah, the Exalted says, «Say 0 men I am sent unto you all as the Messenger of Allah» (158- Al Araf)

And, the Exalted says, :

«We have not sent thee but as a universal Messenger to men giving them glad tidings and warning them (against sin)» (28- Saba)

The Prophet said: «A Prophet was sent to his particular people, but I am sent for all people» (Sahih Al Bukhari 1/86)

And the Prophet said: «By Allah, no one of this nation either Jewish or Christian, who dies without believing in what I was sent for, surely he will be sent to the hell». (Sahih Muslim, Hadith No. 153)

Even his mission covered the Jinn also.

«Behold we turned towards thee a company of Jinns quietly listening to the Quran when they stood in the presence thereof, they said listen in silence when the reading was finished they returned to their people to warn them of their sins».

(29- Al Ahqaf)

«They said, 0 our people we have heard a book revealed after Mosa confirming what came before it; it guides men to the truth and to a straight path»

(30- Al Ahqaf)

«0 our people, hearken to the one who invites you to Allah and believe in him, He will forgive you your faults, and deliver you from a penalty grievous».

(31Al Ahqaf)

«If any does not hearken to the one who invites us to Allah, he cannot frustrate Allah's plan on earth and no protectors can be have besides Allah such men wander in manifest error». (32- Al Ahqaf)

Believing that the Prophet is servant of Allah, not to be worshiped and to believe that he tells nothing but the truth. To believe that he is the last of Prophets and Messengers, and The Holy Quran is the last prevailing Book and superseding all previous faiths.

Allah, the Exalted says: «Muhammad is not the father of any of your men but he is the Messenger of Allah and the seal of the Prophets and Allah has full knowledge of all things» (40- Al Ahzab)

And, the Exalted says: «Those who follow the Messenger the unlettered Prophet whom they find mentioned in their own scriptures in the law and the gospel for he commands them what is evil; he allows them as lawful what is good and pure and prohibits them from what is bad and impure he releases them from their heavy burdens and from the yokes» (157- Al Araf)

And He says: «If anyone desires a religion other than Islam submission to Allah never will it be accepted of him; and in the hereafter he will be in the ranks of those who have lost all spiritual good». (85- Ali Imran)

Muslims believe unanimously in the Prophet and the verses confirmed that expressly.

Allah, the Exalted says: «0 mankind the Messenger hath come to you in truth from Allah, believe in him it is best for you» (170 Al Nisa)

And He says: «0 ye who believe! Believe in Allah and his Messenger and the scripture which he sent to his

Messenger» (136- Al Nisa)

Allah took the covenant of the Prophets to believe in him and to render help to him and if they were alive they would follow him.

Allah, the Glorious says: «Behold! Allah took the covenant of the Prophets saying,

I give you a book and wisdom; then comes to you a Messenger confirming what is with you; do you believe in him and render him help, Allah said: do you agree and take this my covenant as binding on you they said we agree he said then bear witness and I am with you among the witnesses» (81 Ali Imran)

«If any turn back after this they are perverted transgressors» (82- Ali Imran)

Declaring the testimony that Muhammad is the Messenger of Allah entails following him and Allah, and Allah coupled obedience to Him with obedience of the Messenger in several verses. Allah the Exalted says: «He who obeys the Messenger obeys Allah» (80- Al Nisa)

And He says: «Say: obey Allah and obey the Messenger» (54- Al Nur)

And He says: «0 ye who believe obey Allah and obey the Messenger and those charged with authority among you» (59- Al Nisa)

And He says: «Say obey Allah and obey the Messenger but if ye turn away he is only responsible for the duty placed on him and ye for that placed on you. If ye obey him he shall be on right guidance. The Messenger's duty is only to preach the clear message» (54- Al Nur)

Allah dignifies who obeys Allah and His Messenger.

Allah the Exalted says: «All who obey Allah and the Messenger are in the company of those on whom is the grace of Allah of the Prophets who teach the sincere lovers of truth the witnesses who testify and the righteous who do good ah what a beautiful fellowship» (69- Al Nisa)

And Allah promised the paradise for those who obey Him and His Messenger.

Allah the Exalted says: «Those who obey Allah and his Messenger will be admitted to gardens with rivers flowing beneath to abide therein forever and that will be the supreme achievement» (13- Al Nisa)

Believing his tidings is the core of the testimony and Allah praised the Muslims who believed the Prophet.

The Exalted Allah says: «And he who brings the truth and he who confirms and supports it such are the men who do right» (33- Al Zumar)

Allah condemned who denied the Prophet and He menaced them with severe punishment.

Allah the Exalted says: «Who then doth more wrong than one who utters a lie concerning Allah, and rejects the truth when it comes to him! Is there not in hell an abode for blasphemers» (32- Al Zumar)

And Allah says to those who deny the tidings of the Prophet: «Leave me alone, to deal with the creature whom I created bare and alone» (11- Al Muddaththir) «To whom I granted resources in abundance» (12- Al Muddaththir) «And sons to be by his side» (13- Al Muddaththir), «To whom I made life smooth and comfortaable» (14- Al Muddaththir), «Yet is he greedy that I should add yet more» (15- Al Muddaththir), «By no means for to our signs he has been refractory» (16- Al Mudddaththir), «Soon will I visit him with a mount of calamities» (17- Al Muddaththir), «For he thought and he plotted» (18- Al Muddaththir), «And woe to him how he plotted» (19- Al Muddaththir)

«Yea woe to him how he plotted» (20- Al Muddaththir), «Then he looked round» (21- Al Muddaththir), «Then he frowned and he scowled» (22- Al Muddaththir), «Then he turned back and was haughty» (23- Al Muddaththir) «Then said he this is nothing but magic derived from of old» (24- Al Muddaththir), «This is nothing but the word of a mortal» (25- Al Muddaththir) «Soon will I cast him into hell-fire» (26- Al Muddaththir)

And Allah threatens who denies the tidings of the Prophets saying:

«Not one of them but rejected the Messengers but my punishment came justly and inevitable on them» (14- Sad)

And Allah, the Exalted says: «Then sent we our Messengers in succession; every time there came to a people their Messenger they accused him of falsehood; so we made them follow each other in punishment we made them as a tale that is told so away with a people that will not believe» (44- Al Muminun)

The evidence of response to his call is the saying of Allah, the Exalted: «0 ye who believe! Give your response to Allah and his Messenger, when he calleth you to that which will give you life» (24- Al Anfal)

Allah threatened who do not respond to the call of the Prophet, saying: «But if they hearken not to thee know that they only follow their own lusts; and who is more astray than one who follows his own lusts devoid of guidance from Allah, for Allah guides not people given to wrongdoing» (50- Al Qasas)

The testimony that Muhammad is the Messenger of Allah includes that loving, supporting and glorifying him after his death means support to his religion.

The proof of loving him, is that he said: «By Allah no one of you shall be believer until he loves me more than his parent and child» (Sahih Al Bukhari 1/9)

And his saying: «who has three things will feel the sweetness of faith: to love Allah and His Messenger more than anything else» (Sahih AL Bukhari narrated by Anas) and Sahih Muslim Hadith No. 43,67, 76).

Allah the Exalted threatened who prefers anything to love of Allah and His Messenger, saying: «Say if it be that your fathers, your sons, your brothers, your mates, or your kindred the wealth that ye have gained the commerce in which ye fear a decline or the dwellings in which ye delight are dearer to you than Allah or his Messenger or the striving in his cause then wait until Allah brinlls about His decision and Allah lluides not the rebellious» .(24- Al Tawbah)

Omar bin Al Khattab said: «By Allah, 0 the Messenger of Allah you are beloved to me more than anything else except myself. The Prophet said: by Allah no one of you will be a believer until he loves me more than himself, Omar said: you are now beloved to me more than myself. The Prophet said: Now Omar» (Sahih Al Bukhari 8/218).

The proof of support, Allah the Exalted says: «He releases them from their heavy burdens and from the yokes that are upon them. So it is those who believe in him, honour him, help him and follow the light which is sent down with him, it is they who will prosper» (157- Al Arat)

And Allah the Exalted says: «We have truly sent thee as a witness as a bringer of glad tidings and as a warner (8- Al Fath) In order that ye 0 men may believe in Allah and his Messenger that ye may assist and honour him and celebrate his praises morning and evening» (9- Al Fath)

And He says: «Then comes to you a Messenger confirming what is with you; do you believe in him and render him help» (81- Ali Imran)

Allah the Exalted praised a group of the believers saying: «Some part is due to the indigent Muhajirs, those who were expelled from their homes and their property while seeking grace from Allah and his good pleasure, and aiding Allah and his Messenger such are indeed the sincere ones» (8- Al Hashr)

And He says: «If ye help not your leader it is no matter for Allah did indeed help him» (40- Al Tawbah)

And He says: «Deem not the summons of the Messenger among yourselves like the summons of one of to another» (63- Al Nur)

The proof of backing is His saying: «Your real friends are no less than Allah, his Messenger, and the fellowship of believes those who establish regular prayers and regular charity and they bow down humbly I worship (55- Al Maidah)

As tot hose who turn for friendship to Allah, his Messenger and the fellowship of believes it is the fellowship of Allah that must certainly triumph»

(56- Al Maidah)

And Allah says: «If the two turn in repentance to him you hearts are indeed so inclined but if ye back up each other against him truly Allah is his protector and

Gabriel and every righteous one among those who believe and furthermore the angels will back him up» (4- Al Tahrim)

This great testimony includes, also, submission to him and accepting his judgement. The proof is his saying: «But no by the Lord they can have no real faith until they make thee judge in all disputes between them and find in their souls no resistance against thy decisions, but accept them with the fullest conviction» (65- Al Nisa)

Allah the Exalted praises the believers saying: «The answer of the believers when summoned to Allah and his Messenger in order that he may judge between them is no other than this they say we hear and we obey it is such as these that will attain felicity». (51- Al Nur)

Allah the Exalted describes the hypocrites who show differently from what they hide: «They say we believe in Allah and in the Messenger and we obey but even after that some of them turn away they are not really believers (47- Al Nur)

When they are summoned to Allah and his Messenger in order that he may judge between them behold some of them decline to come (48- Al Nur)

But if the right is on their side they come to him with all submission

(49- Al Nur)

Is it that there is a disease in their hearts? Or do they doubt, or are they in fear, that Allah and his Messenger will deal unjustly with them? Nay it is they themselves who do wrong» (50- Al Nur)

Allah the Exalted unmark their status saying: «Hast thou not turned thy vision to those who declare that they believe in the revelations that have come to thee and to those before thee their real wish is to resort together for judgement in their disputes to the evil one though they were ordered to reject him but satan's wish is to lead them astray far away from the right (60- Al Nisa) ??

When it is said to them come to what Allah hath revealed and to the Messenger thou seest the hypocrites avert their faces from thee in disgust» (61- Al Nisa)

Accepting the law of Allah and what the Prophet brought is a must for individuals and rulers as it is the core of the two testimonies «No god but Allah and Muhammad is the Messenger of Allah»

This great testimony ordains imitating the Prophet, following his Sunna, preferring it to any other opinion and avoiding disagreement with him.

Allah the Glorious says: «Ye have indeed in the Messenger of Allah a beautiful pattern of conduct for anyone whose hope is in Allah and the final day and who engages much in the praise of Allah» (21- Al Ahzab)

And He says: «So take what the Messenger assigns to you and deny yourselves that which he withholds from you (7- Al Hashr)

Allah the Exalted says: «Say if ye do love Allah follow me Allah will love you and forgive you your sins» (31- Al Imran)

And He says: «If you differ in anything among yourselves refer it to Allah and his Messenger, if ye do believe in Allah and the last day that is best and most suitable for final determination» (59- Al Nisa)

And He says: «0 ye who believe! Put not yourselves forward before Allah and his Messenger; but fear Allah; for Allah is he who hears and knows all things»

(1- Al Hujurat)

And the Exalted says: «It is not fitting for a believer, man or woman when a matter has been decided by Allah and his Messenger to have any option about their decision if anyone disobeys Allah and his Messenger he is indeed on a clearly wrong path» (36- Al Ahzab)

And He says: «Then let those beware who withstand the Messenger's order lest some trial befall them, or a grievous penalty be inflicted on them» (63- Al Nur)

Imam Ahmad, Allah may be pleased with him says: I wonder when people know the right ascription and they go to the opinion of Sufian. Allah, the Glorious says:

« let those beware who withstand the Messenger's order lest some trial befall them, or a grievous penalty be inflicted on them » (63- Al Nur)

What is trail? It is joining a partner with Allah. Allah the Exalted says: « If any one contends with the Messenger even after guidance has been plainly conveyed to him and follows a path other than that becoming to men of faith we shall leave him in the path he has chosen and land him in hell what an evil refuge»

(115- Al Nisa)

And He says: «This is because they contended against Allah and his Messenger:

If any contend against Allah and his Messenger, Allah is strict in punishment»

(13- Al Anfal)

And He says: «Know they not that for those who oppose Allah and his Messenger, is the fire of hell, wherein they shall dwell. That is the supreme disgrace»

(63- Al Tawbah)

This is the truth of the testimony that Muhammad is the Messenger of Allah in some detail and explanation.

Sheikh Muhammad bin Abdul Wahab, Allah may bestow His mercy upon him, identified it as: obeying his orders, believing his tidings, avoiding his prohibitions and abiding by the laws of Allah.

.

Chapter on the rights of the Prophet over his nation

The Prophet has established rights over his nation including:

- Not to be addressed like common people, but with respect by his title «the Messenger of Allah» or the Prophet of Allah.

Allah the Exalted says: «Deem not the summons of the Messenger among yourselves like the summons of one of you to another» (63- Al Nur)

- To ask the good status for him (Al Wasila).

He says: «Ask for a status to me in the garden, it is a status for one of the servants of Allah, I hope to be that one, and who asks (wasila) for me shall be entitled to intercession».

(Sahih Muslim 1/289) narrated by Abdullah bin Amro bin Al Aas, Allah may be pleased with them.

- To say in the prayers (Allah's blessings and peace be upon him) which some religion scholars considered a basic part for prayer correctness.

Allah the Exalted says: «Allah and his angels send blessings on the Prophet 0 ye that believe send ye blessings on him and salute him with all respect» (56- Al Ahzab)

Chapter on anecdotes about the companions of the Prophet showing how they loved and followed him

Abu Bakr, Allah may be pleased with him was a strong supporter to the Prophet and there are many situations which prove the intensity of his love and faith.

Abi Jaafa Ahmad Al Tabari wrote in his book (Al Riyadh Al Nadhira): «Um Salaama, Allah may be pleased with her said: Abu Bakr was sincere friend of the Prophet. When he was missioned a group of Quraish men went to Abu Bakr and they said: 0 Abu Bakr, your friend has lost his mind. Abu Bakr said: what was his matter? They said: He is there in that mosque calling to monotheism and claiming that he was a Prophet. Abu Bakr went to the Prophet and knocked the door. When he came out, Abu Bakr said: 0 Abul Qasim what I heard about you? He said: «what did you hear Abu Bakr? He said: I heard that you are calling for one Lord and claiming that you are the Prophet of Allah.

The Prophet said: «yes Abu Bakr, my Lord made me bearer of glad tidings and warner to all men». Abu Bakr said: By Lord, I never experienced any lie from you and you are worthy of the mission for your honesty and good deeds. Stretch your hand, to pledge my allegiance to you. The Prophet stretched his hand and Abu Bakr pledged his allegiance and acknowledged that what he brought was the righteous, and he never hesitated when the Messenger of Allah called him.

Al Hakim reported in his (Mustadrak) that Aisha, Allah may be pleased with her said: when the Prophet was taken for a journey at night to the Farthest Mosque, people were talking about it in the morning and some of those who believed in him apostatized and they went to Abu Bakr and said to him: your friend alleges that he was taken for a night journey to the Farthest Mosque. He said: Did he say that? They said: yes. He said: if the Prophet said that he was true. They said: Do you believe him? He said I do believe him on more than that. So he was called Abu Bakr Siddique.

During the immigration (Hijra) the Prophet and Abu Bakr sat in Thawr cave and Quraish men were after them and they assigned prizes for who can bring the Prophet. The men of Quarish were around the cave but they could not see them. Abu Bakr said to the Prophet: By Lord if they looked down they could see us. The Prophet said: *"Allah was the third with us."*

In this Allah, the Exalted says: «If ye help not your leader if is no matter for Allah did indeed help him, when the unbelievers drove him out, he had no more than one companion, the two were in the cave, and he said to his companion, have no fear for Allah is with us, then Allah sent down his peace upon him, and strengthened him with forces which ye saw not, and humbled to the depths the word of the unbelievers but the word of Allah is exalted to the heights for Allah is exalted in might wise». (40- Al Tawbah)

Ibi Hurairah narrated that the Prophet said on Khaibar day: «I will give this flag to a man who loves Allah and His Messenger so that Allah will bring victory at his hands». Omar ibn Al Khattab said: I did not like leadership except on that day. He said: I was expecting to be called for that, but the Prophet called Ali bin Abi Talib and he gave him the flag and said: walk on and do not refrain until Allah gives you the victory. He said: Ali walked some distance then he stopped and cried: 0 the Messenger of Allah, what for I fight people? He said: «fight them until they declare that there is no god but Allah and Muhammad is the Messenger of Allah, if they did so they have protected themselves and their properties and their judgement will be to Allah».

Sahih Al Bukhari - Hadith No. 2405

When the Prophet set out in the company of more than one thousand of his companions in the year of Al Hudaibiya, Orwa bin Masoud Al Thaqafi who was polytheist at that time, when he came back to Quraish he told them: «0 people, I saw kings, I saw Caesar, Chosroes and Najashi, but I did not see a king glorified by his people as Muhammad is glorified by his companions, if he orders them they run to satisfy his order, if he talks they lower their voices and they never stare at him in esteem for him».

(Sahih Al Bukhari 3/178 - 184)

These are some of the magnificent pictures that indicate the great love of the companions of the Prophet and their interest to follow his orders and to submit to him.

This is in brief and there are many great events stated in the books of history that show our good ancestors whom we should follow in knowing the right of the Prophet and in applying his rules.

Chapter on some of those who violate the testimony that Muhammad is the Messenger of Allah

O brothers in Allah, we showed before that who is bound to the fact that Muhammad is the Messenger of Allah apparently and overtly is the true believer and who violates it will be in great danger.

The violators of this testimony are different types:

Some who do not believe in the mission of Muhammad totally such as the polytheists.

Some deny the generality of the mission of the Prophet and say it is assigned to the Arabs only.

Allah the Exalted says: «We have not sent thee but as a universal Messenger to men, giving them glad tidings, and warning them against sin, but most men understand not». (28- Saba)

And He says: «Say: 0 men, I am sent unto you all as the Messenger of Allah».

(158- Al Araf)

And He says: «We know indeed the grief which their words do cause thee it is not thee they reject it is the signs of Allah which the wicked condemn».

(33- Al Anam)

Some testify that Muhammad is the Messenger of Allah and attach themselves to Islam, but they violate it by perpetrating various violations, each bigger than the other.

Some exaggerate and consider him an eternal light moving into the Prophets, and some claim that Allah is manifested through him (we invoke Allah for protection).

The first: Is the saying of the extremist Shiites, Mystics and Sufists.

The second: Is the saying of the people of the (unity of the universe).

All these sayings are atheistic, covered with Islamic dress, misleading and not different from the Christians belief that Essa is The Lord's incarnate.

The Prophet is a human being, servant of Allah and Allah selected him and dignified him to be the last of the Prophets and Messengers. He is the Master of Adam's offspring and being a human being negates all of the said untrue sayings.

Allah, the Exalted says: «Say: I am but a man like yourselves but the inspiration has come to me, that your God is one God whoever expects to meet his Lord, let him work righteousness, and in the worship of his Lord admit no one as partner».

(110- Al Kahf)

And Allah, the Exalted says: « Say: Glory to my Lord, am I aught but a man a Messenger (93- Al Isra)

The Prophet said: «I am a human being like you, I forget as you forget» (Sahih Al Bukhari 1/104,105) and Sahih Muslim 1/402 Hadith No. (572) (92)

These proofs indicate absolutely that Muhammad is a human being and exaggerating his status is against the truth of his mission and contradicts with the testimony that «Muhammad is the Messenger of Allah».

Some exaggerated also by allocating worship to him, such as invocation, humbleness and praying to his grave etc.

The Prophet warned his nation against that and stressed that worship is for Allah alone.

Allah, the Exalted says: «And your Lord says: Call on me; I will answer your prayer but those who are too arrogant to serve me will surely find themselves in hell in humiliation» (60- Ghafir)

And Allah the Exalted says: «These three were ever quick in emulation in good works; they used to call on us with love and reverence and humble themselves before us». (90- Al Anbiya)

Allah the Exalted says to His Messenger: «Therefore to thy Lord turn in prayer and sacrifice» (2- Al Kawthar)

And He says ordering His Prophet: "Say: «truly, my prayer and my service of sacrifice, my life and my death are (all) for Allah the cherisher of the worlds»

(162- Al Anam)

Omar ibn Al Khattab narrated that the Prophet said: «Do not describe me as the Christians described the son of Mariam (Mary), but I am his servant. Say: The servant and Messenger of Allah». (Sahih Al Bukhari 4/142)

Aisha, Allah may be pleased with her said: «The Prophet in his fatal illness said, Allah cursed the Jews and the Christians because they took the graves of their Prophets as places of worship». Aisha added «Had it not been for that the grave of the Prophet would have been prominent but I am afraid it might be taken as a mosque». (Sahih Al Bukhari)

The Prophet strongly prohibited taking the graves as mosques and he cursed who did that, or who invoke the dead people or ask them for benefit or driving away harm.

Al Qurtubi, Allah may bestow His mercy upon him said: Therefore Muslims exaggerated in prohibiting what may lead to sin, and they raised the walls of his grave and blocked the entrances to it. As well they deviated its walls so that it may not be taken as a direction for prayer.

(Al Mofhim book of Imam Qurtabi 2/128)

Thus, Allah the Exalted protected his grave in response to his invocation «0 Lord allow not taking my grave as a worshipped idol».

Another party exaggerated and claimed that the Prophet knows the unseen which is denial to the Book of Allah and atheism.

Allah, the Exalted says: «Say: none in the heavens or in the earth, except Allah knows what is hidden, nor can they perceive when they shall be raised up for judgements» (65- Al Naml)

And Allah, the Exalted says: «To Allah do belong the unseen secrets of the heavens and the earth». (123- Hud)

And He says: «He knoweth the unseen and that which is open; he is the great the most high» (9- Al Rad)

Allah, the Exalted orders His Prophet: Say: «I tell you not that with me are the treasures of Allah, nor do I know what is hidden» (50- Al Anam)

And Allah the Exalted orders His Prophet: «Say: I have no power over any good or harm to myself except as Allah willeth. If I had knowledge of the unseen, I should have multiplied all good, and no evil should have touched me; I am but a warner, and a bringer of glad tidings to those who have faith». (188- Al Araf)

As for the proofs of his death they are many.

Allah, the Exalted says: «Truly thou wilt die one day, and truly they too will die one day». (30- Al Zumar)

«We granted not to any man before thee permanent life (Here) if then thou shouldst die, would they live permanently?» (34- Al Anbiya)

«Every soul shall have a taste of death» (Ali Imran -185)

Aisha narrated the story of his death, at the end of which he said, «The highest compassions» then he passed away. (Sahih Al Bukhari 5/138, 139)

Some people cast doubts about some Hadiths of the Prophet claiming that mind may not accept them, but mind may not contradict with proven report. Imam Shafie, Allah may bestow His mercy upon him said: the scholars of religion agreed unanimously that who verifies the Sunna of the Messenger of Allah should not acccept the sayings of others about it.

Allah, the Exalted says:

«And pursue not that of which thou hast no knowledge; for every act of hearing or of seeing or of feeling in the heart will be enquired into on the day of reckoning» (36- Al Isra)

«Say: the things that my Lord hath indeed forbidden are, shameful deeds, whether open or secret; sins and trespasses against truth or reason assigning of partners to Allah, for which he hath given no authority; and saying things about Allah of which he have no knowledge» (33- Al Araf)

Swearing by the Prophet is minor polytheism and leads to major polytheism The Prophet says: Who swears by other than Allah, he disbelieved in Allah or associated partners with Allah» (Sunan Abi Dawoud 3/570) Hadith No. 3251

Some people violate the testimony of Muhammad is the Messenger of Allah by originating heresies in religion as the faith is to worship Allah only by what the Messenger of Allah brought.

A chapter on the judgement on celebrating the Prophet's birthday

One of the common heresies these days among the Muslims their celebration on the Prophet's birthday especially in the month of Rabi I. On this we say seeking the guidance of Allah:

The origin of this religion is Quran and Sunna(the Prophet's practice). Thus the scholar of religion call for strictness in the acts of worship, which means that a Muslim may approach Allah, the Exalted, only according to His Law and to the Sunna of His Messenger.

Who approaches Allah with deeds he thinks good or took it from others, even from scholars, his deed is heresy although he intended blessing.

Islamic scholars know that as a divine rule when there is difference on a matter it must be referred to the Quran and Sunna. What is provided for we take and what is not provided for we shall not approach Allah through it.

If you differ in anything among yourselves, refer it to Allah and his Messenger, if ye do believe in Allah and the last day that is best and most suitable for final determination. (59- Al Nisa)

And Allah, the Exalted says: «So take what the Messenger assigns to you, and deny yourselves that which he withholds from you» (7- Al Hashr)

Aisha, Allah may bestow His mercy on her, narrated that the Prophet said: «who does a deed which is not our command it is rejected» (Sahih Al Bukhari 8/156 and Sahih Muslim, Hadith No. 1718)

171

Now, we go back to the matter of the Prophet's birthday and say:

Since some scholars approbated it and some scholars described it as heresy, then it is a disputed matter, which must be referred to the Quran and Sunna. If we refer to the Book of Allah we find no basis to support it, and if we trace the autobiography of the Prophet no one reported that the Prophet commanded celebrating his birth day or that somebody celebrated it during his life and he agreed to it, although he lived 63 years and was accompanied by most loving companions who sacrificed themselves defending him, such celebration could not had happened in his time without informing it.

No one of the closest companions of the Prophet; Abu Bakr Al Siddiq, Omar Al Farouq, Othman Thu Al Noorain or Ali (his son-in-law and cousin) narrated that they celebrated the birthday of the Prophet.

Be sure that they left it because there was no basis for it either in the Quran or Sunna, it is just a heresy which the best man left and the best scholars of the nation during the first era of Islam left it. This is a convincing evidence for those who Allah bestows His grace upon them and illuminate their minds.

Celebration of the Prophet's birthday happened in the 4th century by the Fatimids who proved to the Islamic scholars that they were astray group, besides they have atheist opinions, acts and heresies, which disqualifies them to be imitated.

Allah, the Exalted says: «This day have I perfected your religion for you completed my favour upon you and have chosen for you Islam as your religion».

(3- Al Maidah)

Originating such event includes indication that the religion was not completed, which contradicts with the expressed meanings of the Quran.

The Prophet says: «All Prophets before me had to tell their nations the best they knew» (Sahih Muslim - Hadith No. 1844)

Our Prophet, Muhammad was certainly the last and best Prophet. He was the true advisor and the most eloquent. If celebration of his birthday were beneficial to his nation, he would have taken the initiative to urge us to do it. Then we ask those who want to celebrate the Prophet's birthday, on what day, should we celebrate? The experts of the Prophet's autobiography differ on his birthday. Some say its was in Ramadan, some say on 8th of Rabi I and some say it was on 1st of Rabi I. So how can you celebrate?

It is said, also, assume that his birth was in Rabi I, his death was in Rabi I too. Thus, it is worthier to be sad for his death rather than to be happy for his birth.

Such celebrations include blights and causes of corruption on basis of the following:

Believing that this celebration is an approach to Allah and the rule on this is strictness in accepting acts of worship and there is no evidence for that.

It includes doctrinal wrongdoings and ethical evil: The doctrinal wrong doings are the exaggerated praise, which reaches divinity and allocation of invocation to him.

The ethical wrong doings include mixing of both sexes dancing until late hours of night, which suits the wicked ones.

Some accused who do not celebrate this occasion with atheism.

Certainly, this is a temptation by Satan and this is a detestable heresy.

Some of them quote the verse: «Say: in the bounty of Allah and in his mercy in that let them rejoice» (58- Yunus)

They say rejoice with the Prophet is commanded by Allah.

We comment on that seeking the guidance of Allah:

First: Such indication was not said by the good ancestors and if it was good, they would have preceded us to it. The interpretation of the ancestors to this verse is that the mercy of Allah is meant to be the Islam and Sunna.

Some of them may have relied to the Hadith reported by Baihaqi that Anas said:

«The Prophet offered a birth sacrifice for himself"

This Hadith is frail and denied by the scholars of religion. Malik commented when he was asked about this Hadith: (Did you see the companions of the Prophet who did not sacrifice before Islam, did they sacrifice for themselves after Islam? These are vanities).

(See the book of Ibin Rushd «AI Mokaddimat»)

In (Masael Abi Dawoud): That Ahmad when he reported this Hadith he said: It is trail and denied.

Al Baihaqi, Allah may bestow His mercy upon him, the Hadith reporter said:

Abdulla bin Muharrar narrated on the birth sacrifice of the Prophet by himself that it was disregarded Hadith and he mentioned the Hadith with its references and it is reported that Anas said, it is not authentic.

(Al Sunan Al Kubra - Al Baihaqi)

Nawawi, Allah may bestow His mercy upon him, also decided that this Hadith was null. So their inference is obvious omission.

They have also other inferences without support, but as Allah, the Exalted says:

«They follow nothing but conjecture and what their own souls desire, even though there has already come to them guidance from their Lord». (23- Al Najm)

Accordingly, such ceremonies are heresies, without clear argument and imitation to the astray Nazarenes in increasing their festivals, which indicates weak religion and knowledge.

The Prophet told us: «Surely you will follow the ways of those nations who were before you, span by span and cubit by cubit so much so that even if they entered a hole of mastigar, you would follow them». (Sahih Al Bukhari - after Abi Saeed Al Khidri, Allah may be pleased with him) we ask Allah to lead us and all Muslims to the righteous way»

His word ended.

The assignment of the Prophets

The need of human beings to divine messages is more than the need of a patient to a doctor.

The absence of a doctor entails at the worst damage to the body, but absence of the divine message entails heart damage and there is no survival to the people of the earth if they do not carry the effects of the divine message. When this message effects vanish from the earth Allah commands the great rising.

Shaikh Dr. Saleh bin Fouzan bin Abdullah

Al Fouzan Guidance to righteous belief and replying to the polytheists

The meaning of «Muhammad is the Messenger of Allah»

Chapter on the meaning of the testimony that Muhammad is the Messenger of Allah

Question: What is the meaning of the testimony that Muhammad is the Messenger? of Allah?

1- Obeying his commands

2- Believing his tidings

3- Avoiding what he prohibited

4- To worship Allah only within His Laws

1- Obeying his commands:

If you believe that Muhammad is the Messenger of Allah, and what he brought is revealed to him by Allah, then you have to obey his orders.

If you do not obey his commands, you have renounced your testimony.

Who says «I declare that Muhammad is the Messenger of Allah » and he believes that obeying the Prophet is unnecessary for him, he is hypocrite.

If you believe that you have to obey the Messenger but you violated his rules forced by your desire then you are disobedient and not completing this testimony.

2- Believing his tidings

What the Prophet told about unseen things, attributes of Allah, paradise and hell are inspiration by Allah.

When you declare that he is the Messenger of Allah you have to believe his tidings and to bear no doubt about what he tells even if you do not see it.

3- Avoiding his prohibitions

What the Prophet prohibits must be avoided for Allah, the Exalted says: «So take what the Messenger assigns to you, and deny yourselves that which he withholds from you» (7- Al Hashr)

The commands and news brought to you by the Messenger are to be taken.

What he prohibits must be avoided in obedience to Allah the Exalted and to His Messenger.

Who neglects avoiding what the Prophet prohibited believing that he is not bound, this is considered calumny in testimony.

Who accepts to abide by the prohibitions of the Prophet but he could not resist himself and committed violation, he is disobedient to Allah and to his Messenger and his testimony is incomplete.

4- To worship Allah only within His Laws.

Not to worship Him with heresies

Worship Him as the Prophet showed.

Worship Allah under one method, the method of the Prophet.

If the Muslim believes truly that Muhammad is the Messenger of Allah then his testimony will be complete and he will be a real Muslim.

* From the tapes «AI Osool Al Thalathi -

Discussion of Shaikh Dr. Saleh Al Shaikh

Chapter Seven
The impact of the testimony
There is no god but Allah

Effects of Completing Monotheism

Sheikh Saleh Al Shaikh, Allah may protect him said in his sermon:

O brother believers, the heart of the believer shall not be sound except with glorifying Allah, the Exalted, and shall not be constant on faith, unless with achieving oneness of Allah, the Glorious. The more the man becomes faithful to Allah and completes the two testimonies; there is no god but Allah and Muhammad is the Messenger of Allah, the more he will be firm in his faith. Allah the Exalted says: «Say: verily, I am commanded to serve Allah with sincere devotion»

(11- Al Zumar)

And He says: «Is it not to Allah that sincere devotion is due?» (3- Al Zumar)

It means worship Allah sincerely, and for that He created Jinn and men. «I have only created Jinns and men, that they may serve Me» (56- Al Dhariyat)

For this great affair, the Fire and the Paradise were created, and for this purpose the flags of Jihad (to strive) were raised and for monotheism Allah granted victory to the faithful.

Thus, the faithful must be sincere in their worship to Allah exclusively, and obedience of the Messenger is obedience to Allah, the Exalted.

«Say: obey Allah and his Messenger, but if they turn back Allah loveth not those who reject faith» (32- Al Imran)

O believers: The faithful man who satisfies monotheism he will be blessed by Allah in life and in the hereafter. Thus, Allah the Glorious, confirmed to his faithful servants, that monotheism is the greatest thing that draw the servant close to his Lord. Allah, the Exalted says: «It is those who believe and confuse not their beliefs with wrong that are truly in security, for they are on right guidance» (82- Al Anam)

When this verse was revealed to the companions of the Prophet they found it difficult for them and they said: 0 the Messenger of Allah, who of us confuses not his belief? «He said: «you do not mean by confusion joining partners with Allah. Didn't you hear the saying of the good servant» Do not join partners with Allah, polytheism is great wrong-doing».

(Reported by Al Bukhari 4776 and Muslim 124, narrated by Abdulla bin Masoud)

Allah, the Exalted promises his servants who are far away from polytheism, that they will have security in life and in the hereafter.

«It is those who believe and confuse not their beliefs with wrong that are truly in security, for they are on right guidance» (82- Al Anam)

The advantage of monotheism is that the more you devote your loyalty to Allah and avoid polytheism apparently and overtly the more security you will have in life and in the hereafter. Allah, the Glorious says: «The great terror will bring them no grief; but the angels will meet them with mutual greetings this is your day the day that ye were promised» (103- Al Anbiya)

Yes the true believer will not fear people in life because he has loyalty to Allah that makes him secure and he will not fear the hell. «Not the slightest sound will they hear of hell; what their souls desired in that will they dwell» (102- Al Anbiya)

Anas bin Malik narrated that the Prophet said: «Allah the Glorious said «my servant, if you come to me with as much sins as fills the earth, but you meet me without joining partner with me, I will forgive you» (Reported by Tarmathi 3540)

The monotheist, his sins will be forgiven and (there is no god but Allah) will be a card for him on the day of judgement that overweighs the sins scroll in view of its heaviness for who achieves it and behaves according to its conditions.

Allah, the Exalted says: «Thus did we order that we might turn away from him all evil and shameful deeds; for he was one of our servants sincere and purified». (24- Yusuf)

The same verse starts with: «And with passion did she desire him and he would have desired her but that he saw the evidence of his Lord» (24- Yusuf)

There is no doubt that the faithful servant, Allah will drive away obscenity from him. As well monotheists always escape the misfortunes. Allah, the Glorious says: «As to the Thamud we gave them guidance but they preferred blindness of heart to guidance so the sunning punishment of humiliation seized them, because of what they had earned» (17- Fussilat)

«But we delivered those who believed and practiced righteousness» (18Fussilat)

Monotheists if they suffer as the others suffer they will escape in the hereafter and the wrong-doing people will be punished in the earthly life and in the hereafter. Allah, the Exalted says: «And we saved those who believed and practiced righteousness» (53- Al Naml)

O believer, know that Allah, the Glorious, will not forgive who joins partner with Him.

«Allah forgiveth not the sin of joining other gods with him, but he forgiveth whom he pleaseth other sins than this; one who joins other gods with Allah hath strayed far, far away from the right». (116- Al Nisa)

The punishment for polytheists is humiliation in the earthly life and hell in the hereafter. «If anyone assigns partners to Allah, he is as if he had fallen from heaven and been snatched up by birds, or the wind had swooped like a bird on its prey and thrown him into a far distant place» (31- Al Hajj)

And the Exalted says: «But said Christ O children of Israel worship Allah my Lord and your Lord whoever joints other gods with Allah, Allah will forbid him the garden and the fire will be his abode. There will for the wrongdoers be no one to help». (72- Al Maidah)

O faithful brothers: As we know that the advantage of monotheism is great, and polytheism punishment is grievous, we need to learn monotheism constantly and turn away from polytheism. If Allah, the Glorious ordered his Prophet to know monotheism we are the more so. «Know therefore, that there is no god but Allah» (19- Muhammad)

Learning monotheism may be generally i.e. to know its judgement, meanings and types and in detail i.e. to learn the matters of monotheism: hope, fear, dependence and turn in repentance to Allah, the Glorious by devoting deeds to Allah.

As well knowing the minor polytheism and the major polytheism, do not say there are known things, Ibrahim (Allah's beloved one) invoked his Lord saying: «Remember Ibrahim said; 0 my Lord make this city one of peace and security; and preserve me and my sons from worshipping idols» (35- Ibrahim)

Therefore, I recommend all to know the speech of the experts in monotheism to win the satisfaction of Allah, to be secure and to drive away the evils.

Listen to Allah, the Exalted says: «Say: He is Allah the one and only» (1- Al Ikhlas) «Allah, the eternal, absolute» (2- Al Ikhlas), «He begetteth not, nor is he begotten» (3- Al Ikhlas), «And there is none like unto Him» (4- Al Ikhlas)

And He says: «Say: 0 ye that reject faith» (1- Al Kafirun), «I worship not that which ye worship» (2- Al Kafirun), «Not will ye worship that which I worship» (3- Al Kafirun), «And I will not worship that which ye have been wont to worship»(4- Al Kafirun), «Not will ye worship that which I worship»(5- Al Kafirun), «To you be your way, and to me mine»(6- Al Kafirun)

The two suras concurred in achieving monotheism and freedom from disbelief. Thus the Prophet was repeating them.

O believers, when you hear this urge you are required to read and hear the expert's discussion for it as this is the way to achieve monotheism.

The Prophet says: «If the first and last of you, your men and Jinn each asked me for a matter and I gave each his matter, my properties will not decrease at all» (Reported by Muslim 2577- after Abi Thar).

Learn the love of Allah and learn oneness of Allah, the former includes love and the latter includes obedience and loyalty and all types of monotheism. (His word ended, Allah may protect him).

The impact of the word (No god but Allah)

1- Actualization of knowing Allah, the Glorious is one of the greatest effects. One may ask: «How can we know Him?»

Ibin Al Qayiem said; this knowledge has two entrances: the first:

Contemplating all verses of the Quran.The second:

Knowing the meanings of Allah's good names.

2- Relaxation and happiness of the monotheist's self as it accepts orders from one source and rejects the prohibitions of one source, which gives tranquility to the mind and heart.

He is known to every sensible person that the mind can not bear orders from several sources.

3- Humbleness of the monotheist and his subjection to the creator and its feeling the need for Him at all times, as He is the Lord and the Director, which enhances the pride of the monotheist to be far above the offers of people.

The creature is weak and poor before the power of Allah the Exalted, the All-Mighty will be pleased and the monotheist feels happy when he subjects himself to the Lord of sovereignty.

4- Certainty and trust in Allah the All-Mighty.

5- Certainty in Allah's support

6- Drive worries away

7 - Seriousness in dealing with matters because the monotheist knows his objective and knows why he was created.

8- Monotheism emancipates the individual from slavery to the creatures. Clinging to them, fearing them and working for them, which embodies the real dignity.

9- It urges the monotheist to perform good deeds and to reject evils.

The monotheist gives priority to obedience of Allah over his sins and it will be easy for him to reject the sins fearing the punishment of Allah.

Allah, the Exalted says: "Thus did we order that we might turn away from him all evil and shameful deeds; for he was one of our servants sincere and purified" (24- Yusuf)

The reason of driving away the obscenity is that he is a sincere servant of Allah.

10- Monotheism illuminates the heart, delights the soul and gives meaning and taste to life.

11- Fairness and habituating self to justice.

12- Eliminating confusion and hesitation

13- Uniting the monotheist Muslims

14- Monotheists are ready to sacrifice money and self for the cause of Allah and backing up his religion.

15- A Monotheists feels that Allah, the All-Mighty is with him and he is not alone.

16- Knowledge and insight. Who knows the reality of monotheism knows polytheism and its fouls.

17- Loving the people of faith and supporting them against the polytheists

Monotheism imprints effects on the soul of the monotheist and who misses these effects should reconsider his monotheism and inspect himself.

Conclusion

Conclusion

O teachers, fathers and mothers:

Allah, the Exalted says: «And let me not be in disgrace on the day when men will be raised up» (87- Al Shuara)

«The day whereon neither wealth nor sons will avail» (88- Al Shuara)

«But only he will prosper that brings to Allah a sound heart» (89- Al Shuara)

The Prophet said: «There is a morsel in the body, if it is good the whole body will be good, and if it is corrupted, the whole body will be corrupted; it is the heart,» (Reported by Bukhari and Muslim).

Sheikh Saleh bin Hamied, Allah may protect him says: It is worthy brothers «particularly the knowledge seekers» while they are discussing monotheism to the public to urge them to inspect their hearts for complete yield, submission, fear, glorification, love, hope, repentance and true trust in Allah.

All of these are heart deeds and man can test himself.

To what extent are they devoted to Allah, the Exalted?

To what extent are they related to things other than Allah?

To what extent any of these is left to parties other than Allah?

His word, Allah may protect him, ended.

The preacher and educator must consider this matter, which is habituating people to examine their hearts and to call Allah to purify their hearts. As well, the preacher must have in mind, an objective and obligation.

The objective is «purification». Allah, the Exalted says: «truly he succeeds that purifies it» (9- Al Shams)

The soul may not be purified except with purifying the heart.

This is what Shaikh Saleh bin Hamied, Allah may protect him, affirmed, saying:

So long as the heart is full with these meanings of fear, love, glorification, sincere faith in Allah's promise and warning and believing in what the Messengers brought and what the Books revealed - this is monotheism and this is the faith. If the heart is filled with these meanings, it will be reflected on the rest of the organs.

(His word, Allah may protect him, ended).

This great word includes all of these meanings:

* Love

* Fear and hope

* Honor

* Esteem

* Glorification

* Subjection

If the heart is filled with these values, the organs will be directed to worship. We are in the era of lusts and desires. The uncontrolled TV channels stir lusts with those who have weak faith. Save the people and fill their hearts with monotheism - make them love their creator and teach them His attributes, his fear and his hope.

The obligation is to know the Divine Law, applying it, calling for it, endure pain in it and invocation for you and for the Muslims before and after taking lessons of knowledge.

To the preachers

Al Albani, Allah may bestow His mercy upon him, the knowledgeable scholar said: «Many Muslims declare that there is no god but Allah, and Muhammad is the Messenger of Allah, but they are not giving the two testimonies their right, this is a long discussion. And many Muslims today - even some preachers are not giving «there is no god but Allah» it's right of interpretation.

Sheikh Abdul Aziz Al Shaikh says: The stronger monotheism is, the more subjection to Allah's Divine Law will be, and the weaker it is, the less good deeds will be performed. Make monotheism on top of your call; try to explain it to your called people. If they understand monotheism and know its implications, they will be subject to Allah's Divine Law.

Dr. Saleh bin Hamied, Allah may protect him, says: There is another methodical error which is the ancestors, Allah may bestow His mercy upon them, followed in the section of Islam tenets scholastic methods and logical terminology so people were unfamiliar with many of the religion principles, but if they followed the method of Quran in statement, then people will be more fit for the guidance of Allah.

Ibin Hijr Al Haithami, Allah may protect him, says: «Those who promote the science of dialectic theology among the common people should be stopped due to lack of knowledge of the common people and their avoiding astray is not secure. People should be led to the text of Quran as it is clear and understood by intuition».

(Haram Sermon - Monotheism First)

I invoke Allah, the All-Mighty to make this beneficial knowledge for Islam and Muslims.

Rabaa Al Taweel

Index

Reference List

Read sources :

1- The Holy Quran

2- Sahih Al Bukhari

3- Sahih Muslim

4- Fath Al Majeed - Shaikah Abdul Rahman H Al Shaikah

5- Fath Al Majeed - Verification of Muhammad lbrahim Al Qarawi

6- Al Osool Al Thalatha - Shaikh Muhammad bin Abdul Wahab

7 - Al Qawi Al Mufeed - Shaikh Muhammad bin Saleh Al Othmain

8- Minhaj Al Firqa Al Najia - compiled by Muhammad lbin Jarniel Zeno

9- The meaning of no god but Allah and its conditions - Saleh bin Al Olaiwi

10- Ianat Al Mustafied - Shaikh Saleh Al Fouzan

11- The reality of Muhammad is the Messenger of Allah - Shaikh Abdul Aziz Al Shaikh

12- Fiqh Al Adeiya Wal Athkar - Shaikh Abdul Razzaq Al Bader

13- AL Natij Al Asma - Muhammad Al Najdi

Audio Sources :

1- Friday Sermon : Monotheism, Shaikh Abdul Aziz Al Shaikh

2- Tapes of Al Osool Al Thalatha - Dr. Saleh Al Shaikh

3- Commentary on Al Zumar Sura - Shaikh Saleh bin Harnied

4- The fact of «No god but Allah» - Shaikh Saleh Fouzan Al Fouzan